A COMMUNITY APPROACH TO BULLYING

A COMMUNITY APPROACH TO BULLYING

Peter Randall

Trentham Books

First published in 1996 by Trentham Books Limited

Trentham Books Limited
Westview House
734 London Road
Oakhill
Stoke-on-Trent
Staffordshire
England ST4 5NP

British Cataloguing in Publication Data
A catalogue record for this book is available from the British Library
ISBN: 1 85856 060 8

Designed and typeset by Trentham Print Design Ltd., Chester
and printed in Great Britain by BPC Wheatons Ltd., Exeter

Contents

Acknowledgments

A very large vote of thanks must go to those victims of all ages who have brought me their histories of pain, sorrow and distress and allowed me to write about them. That openness takes a special courage which I only wish I could repay properly. They also brought their trust that my colleagues and I could help them and, in so doing, learn to do more to stop bullying. Without them there would be no practical substance to this book or need to write it.

There were also the bullies who, realising that they were becoming their own worst enemies, were not only strong enough to admit their wrong but also help me understand so much better the problems they cause. I am very pleased to offer them my gratitude.

I must thank sincerely the army of lay-people and professionals who have contributed their ideas, energy and enthusiasm to the various projects that have provided the foundations for this book. Without their efforts there could have been no community projects to draw from. I am particularly grateful to Humberside County Council and Hull Safer Cities for financial support and encouragement.

But without doubt, the person to whom I must give my greatest thanks is Mike Donohue whose skills, humanity and passionate advocacy for victims have been incredible. He took our ideas and project design and turned them into a working service that has given back the self-esteem, confidence and sense of security to hundreds of people each year. Now the Chief Executive of the Community Anti-Bullying Project, a national charity rapidly achieving international acclaim, Mike has earned my total respect and I look forward to years more work with him.

Preface

There is a dangerous myth circulating amongst confident adults that bullying is a kids' game played in school and if ever adults do complain of being bullied or victimised or harassed, then they are just weak people who can't take pressure. Yet those who work with the victims of bullying realise that this is a problem that can happen to anyone at any age, within any social environment from the home to the workplace, and that it is as old as the human race. Unless the myth is dispelled society will continue to condone by passivity and ignorance one of the most common and destructive forms of power abuse.

Part of the myth is that bullying is born within schools and that teachers are the ones who must take the lead in stopping it. There is little understanding that bullying is usually a problem incubated within local communities and refined by the behaviour of hostile adults whose model of aggression is a potent sculptor of developing young minds. It is at this level that we should intervene and try to stop a process through which children become bullies whose motivations are contrary to those required by a truly civilised society.

From these considerations, I began to develop my ideas about community approaches to bullying in which schools, as part of the community, could take part; an inversion of the more usual schools-based projects which might involve the community at a superficial level. This book is about the design and structure of such a project and details how it may be replicated. Data is still being gathered but indications are that a reduction of 30-50% of bullying across a targeted community may be expected after two years. This translates into the release from fear and shame of hundreds of victims of all ages as well as a great increase in the awareness and skills of professionals who work within the schools, health centres and social services offices of the community. I hope sincerely that the efforts my colleagues and I have made in this work will be of assistance to other people who work to reduce bullying and thus to many other communities.

Peter Randall, The University of Hull
March 1996

CHAPTER I

Schools are not to blame

During the course of the late eighties and early nineties the mass media paraded an endless succession of victims of bullying. Although a handful had been in the armed forces or prison, the vast majority were school pupils. The way the media has handled these situations, including the 'responsible" press, has given the impression that these incidents of bullying have been the product of school difficulties and teacher ineptitude. The implication is that schools are in some ways to blame for the bullying, that teachers create environments in which children learn to subjugate others and make prisoners of them in their classes.

A few examples drawn from the headlines of some local papers from around the country show this representation of bullying:

THE SCHOOL OF HARD KNOCKS
SCHOOL FOR THUGS
TEACHERS FAIL VICTIMS OF BULLYING
|SCHOOLS URGED TO OWN UP TO BULLYING
SUFFER LITTLE CHILDREN – AT SCHOOL

The following is a part of one story that appeared in a local newspaper and had a profoundly negative effect on a primary school that served the same community. Notice how it attacks the school but fails to pick up on the clues that the real reasons of the reported bullying lay elsewhere:

'Our reporter was told by Mrs. P., Jane's mother, that the teachers had completely failed to pick up the signs of Jane's distress at school.

'They didn't see how unhappy she was and when they did, they did nothing about it. They were worse than useless — I'm keeping her at home with me now'. Unfortunately the Headteacher, Mr. B., was unavailable for comment.

Mr.s P., whose home had been wrecked last year by mystery neighbours, is going to take her complaints about the school to...'

The reporter never wondered why Mrs. P. herself hadn't spotted her daughter's distress and failed to examine the possible link between Jane's bullying and the vandalism. On further examination this was a very clear case of fierce arguments between neighbours being picked up by children and carried over in to the school.

The reality of bullying, therefore, is often a long way from the over-simplistic analysis that the media represent. It is the writer's experience that schools do not create bullying; at best they merely import it from the communities they serve, at worst they allow it to flourish by not giving it the constant attention it deserves.

This chapter expands on this argument and does so in relation to available research information and case study examples drawn from large projects that the writer has been involved with since 1991. Evidence will be presented that bullying is experienced by schools in much the same way that vandalism, theft and drug abuse are experienced, the less pleasant faces of community life surrounding its youngest members. Before this, though, it is necessary to define what is meant by bullying in relation to the context of the community.

Bullying: What is it really?

It seems that the authors of every book on the subject of bullying ask this question or one like it. There is a very good reason for this. It is incumbent upon authors to make sure that their readers know exactly what the book is about, and share the same concept of the topic before moving on through the material the book presents. A lack of initial common under-standing often leads to confusion, misunderstanding and disappointment.

The problem is, however, that agreed definitions of bullying are hard to find. Although adults have their own ideas about what bullying is, there is often considerable disparity between them. A common mistake is to believe that it is good enough to say 'Bullying is ...' followed by a list of bullying-behaviours. A group of 6 years old children told me that bullying is:

'... when they bang me against the wall and kick me',
'... the way they call me names like scumbag',
'... standing close to me and looking tough',
'... taking me lunch off me and standing on it',
'... saying my Mom's a slag',
'... saying I'm a rotten footballer and not letting me play with them',
'... spitting on my new coat'.

Older children hold a similar opinion of bullying as these 15 year old pupils reveal

'Bullying in our school is all about beating people up',
'It's making the weak ones cough up' (money, sweets, etc).
'... telling tales about me and my boyfriend — I'm not a tart'.
'It's throwing my stuff out of the window every day'.

Adults also take much the same view as this sample of people in one community described:-

'Bullying is when the S—— family shout bad language at us in the street',
'It happens to me when I get dog muck through the letter box',
'At work it happens when the charge hand makes me look small in front of all the other women'.
'It's all about beating up the Asians on the estate'.

We can see from these descriptions that children, adolescents and adults take note of certain behaviours they witness and pin a generic label on them — bullying. But all these descriptions do not actually tell us what bullying is — only how it is demonstrated. Even when we examine the definitions given by experts in the field we still find there are significant differences. Take these as examples:

'A student is being bullied or victimised when he or she is exposed, repeatedly and over time, to negative actions on the part of one or more students' (Olweus, 1986).

'Bullying can be described as the systematic abuse of power' (Smith and Sharp, 1994).

'Bullying is repeated aggression, verbal, psychological or physical, conducted by an individual or group against others' (Guidelines on Countering Bullying Behaviour in Primary and Post-Primary Schools, 1993).

Clearly there are similarities between these three definitions but they are not identical. From them all we gain is a sense that bullying is repeated or systematic, it is not just a one-off act but is a succession of events that are intrinsically aggressive.

Yet there is more to bullying than the characteristic of repeated aggression. There is also intention (Chazan, 1989); specifically the intention to inflict pain in whatever form the bully selects. To make this point it helps to take some instances of aggressive actions.

In the first case a 34 year old man, Paul, has had yet another row with his wife before going to work. He is angry and bitter, frustrated by his inability to stop the arguments. Paul arrives at work wearing a frown and carrying his anger like a badge. His secretary has made some errors in his appointments and he bangs around and shouts impulsively at her, his annoyance at his wife translated into the oppression of another person. Later he apologises for his actions and promises not to be like that again.

Do we regard this man's behaviour as bullying? Probably not. The key to the understanding of his behaviour lies in use of the word 'impulsively', his aggression is unthinking and of the moment. Even if he is often like this, frustrated and bad tempered, we are hardly likely to believe that he *wants* to inflict pain on his secretary. Now examine this example.

Thirteen year old Kevin has a long history of being aggressive that dates back to the time he spent in a nursery class. Over the years his aggression has become quite devious. He now has a small gang of admirers who, on his instructions, will physically intimidate various 'soft targets' to extract money, sweets and toys from them. Kevin sells the sweets in his own school and gets his younger brother, Tim, to sell the toys in the primary school he attends.

Do we regard Kevin's activities as bullying? Most people asked in a test carried out by the writer (Randall, 1995) either decided immediately that this was bullying or did so after a period of reflection. They recognised that although Kevin does not actually do the 'dirty work' himself, he nevertheless instigates it and profits from it.

The difference between the case studies of Paul and Kevin should be immediately obvious. Paul is impulsively aggressive and subsequently acknowledges the pain he has caused. Kevin, on the other hand, is intentionally aggressive and uses the fear of pain for his own ends, in this case, extortion.

It is possible to analyse many instances of human aggression in this way and to arrive at the conclusion that, whatever else bullying may be and whatever form it make take, bullies are always aggressive individuals who *intend* to cause pain or the fear of pain (Randall, 1991). This does not mean that all aggressive people are bullies, indeed Paul described above is not; it does, however, acknowledge the fact that there are no bullies who are not aggressive because, as we have seen, bullying is a virulent form of aggression. It is for this reason that the operational definition of bullying guiding this book is:

> Bullying is the aggressive behaviour arising from the deliberate intent to cause physical or psychological distress to others.

Notice that this definition emphasises the issues of aggression and intent but does not mention that of regularity or repetition that is mentioned in other definitions given previously.

There is a good reason for this. Aggressive behaviour does not have to be regular or repeated for it to be bullying behaviour. Take this example given to me by a 25 year old ex-convict from a prison in New York State.

> 'It only happened once. That was three days after I arrived. He waited until the end of the exercise period when we were all coming back in from the yard. As soon as the guards couldn't see us, he grabbed me, threw me down and kicked me in the back and stomach three times. 'That's just to let you know who's boss', he said and then walked off. I didn't need telling again and did whatever he wanted afterwards'.

This is clearly an incident of bullying behaviour and yet it occurred on only one occasion to this victim. In response to this people often argue that it is the fear of repeated aggression that is important, not the actual incidence. This is true in many cases as victims often point out, but this is more a characteristic of victims and their understanding of the bullies' personalities than that of the behaviour itself.

Brendan Bryne makes a useful contribution to this discussion by also providing definitions of *Bullies and Victims*;

> 'Bully: A boy or girl who fairly often oppresses or harasses somebody else. The targets may be boys or girls, the harassment physical or mental.

Victim: A boy or girl who for a fairly long time has been and still is exposed to aggression from others ...' (Bryne, 1994, p.20).

We can see here where the issue of repetition is properly located, in the behaviour of the bully and the experiences of the victim.

So, bullying is an intentionally aggressive behaviour carried out by people who are likely to repeat this behaviour regularly. The following examples of bullying recounted by victims of all ages and walks of life show both the intentional and aggressive characteristics of bullying over a very wide range of this behaviour:

'As soon as they found out I couldn't see very well, they started taking my things and hiding them. It's being going on for years now. When I start looking they sing 'Bottle Bottom's on the trail again' and slap me with rulers' (*9 year old boy in an independent school called Bottle Bottom because of the very thick lens glasses he wears*).

'Jackie was my best friend. Then we fell out over something silly. She started telling tales about me to her friends and said 'Pass it on'. Now everywhere I go I get called 'Slag' and 'Whore'. My Mum has started to believe it — I feel so cheap' (*15 year old girl in a mixed sex comprehensive school*).

'Robbie's the gang leader. He really likes to hurt you. But he knows how to hurt so it don't leave bruises, he and his mates just sort of slap and jab you. They got me three times last week and God know how many other kids as well. The teachers have caught him but he just says 'we were only larking about — look, there is no mark'. If you don't agree with him you just get filled in later'. (*15 years old boy in a single sex comprehensive school*).

'She's dead clever is our charge hand. The management thinks she is a real good supervisor but she's got us all terrified. As far as I know she's never hurt anyone but she's so threatening. She's spooky just like that psycho in 'Silence of the Lambs' — she's only got to stand beside me and start whispering about how she's going to fix me up and how her family like to hold grudges, and I nearly piss myself. Every week its something different, like going on unpopular shifts or taking on some of her packaging work which she hates — she is really clever, never leaves any proof' (*32 year old fish process worker*).

'He's an absolute bastard. He always chases the office girls, barking orders at them. Me, he doesn't shout at. But he gets me in other ways — blocking my holiday dates and complaining about the standard of my work. I was late once, only 10 minutes, when my husband was ill and he keeps saying that he's put 'Bad timekeeper' on my personnel record. I have complained about it to the Equal Ops. people in the Council but they say unless someone else will support me there's no case to answer'. (*29 year old finance officer for a local authority*).

'I'm the only Chinese kid in the school. Some of the black kids quickly began calling me 'Snake Eyes'. They went round saying that my mother smells of chip fat and soy sauce which stopped nice kids from coming home with me' (*eleven year old Chinese boy from a 'Take-Away' shop attending Year 6 of primary school*).

'My deformed spine makes me all bent over and doubled up. Some of the girls started calling me 'Quasy' after the Hunchback, then they started saying my father buggers me standing up. I complained to the teacher but she thought I was lying 'cos one of the kids is the daughter of a friend of hers who is teaching in another school ...' (*14 year old boy attending a mixed comprehensive*).

'I know I'm fat but why do people have to keep mentioning everyday whenever there's no one around to hear them. I don't smell but they say I do — God, I'm cleaner than they are. Yet, if I made any catty sexist remarks about women they'd by straight off to Personnel to complain' (*23 year old man working in an otherwise all-women grant processing office*).

'I was slagged off about my parents after they separated. My Dad must have chased after every woman on the estate. The only person who didn't know was my Mom. Now the kids keep saying I'm chasing their sisters; several times four of them beat me up because I was once talking to a girl they fancied. They always trap me on the way home when no-one sees', (*13 year old boy from a mixed comprehensive school*).

These examples show clearly the aggression that underpins the bullying and the repetitive nature of the problem as perceived by the victims. In this case of pupils, they also show that the original causes of the bullying often emanate from outside of schools.

The reasons for this generally have to do with the characteristics of bullies and victims as this review demonstrates.

Characteristics of Bullies

Olweus (1993) makes the point that a distinct characteristic of bullies is their aggression towards their peers. This aggression may well also be directed towards adults such as parents as well as peers and may well have been a consistent trait from infancy. Amongst their other negative traits is a lack of empathy for their victims and a strong need to dominate them (Olweus, 1978). Olweus also lists impulsivity, greater physical strength than the norm for their age and a positive attitude towards violence.

Bullies do not appear to suffer significantly from social anxiety or low self-esteem (Pulkkinen and Tremblay, 1992). Neither are they particularly unpopular (Olweus, 1978, Pulkkinen and Tremblay, 1992). Many have a small coterie of admirers who respect and possibly wish to be like them (Cairns, Cairns, Neckermann, Gest and Gariépy, 1988) and become 'passive bullies' (Olweus, 1993)

Many bullies show evidence of having aggressive conduct disorders from their preschool years (Randall, 1994) and although there may be a constitutional basis for some it is more likely for the majority that family influences are responsible (eg. Olweus, 1993). Several studies (eg. Bowers, Smith and Binney, 1992), have found that, in comparison to controls, bullies perceive their families as lacking in affection and as failing to monitor their behaviour successfully. Power struggles are also common within their families with other siblings. Adolescents who are regularly both bullies and victims complain of excessive *punitiveness* and low levels of positive involvement.

These issues are not simple and a whole variety of family factors are associated with the creation of aggressive conduct disorders. In one recent study of the relationship of adolescent bullying to family functioning (Rigby, 1994) there was a clear finding that adolescents who experienced low levels of emotional support and, whose families were not sympathetic and understanding when they felt sad, were more likely to bully their peers. In addition, however, Rigby makes the points that it is not just a matter of parental attitude but the family situation in toto. The skill of the family in sustaining positive and effective communication is seen as being a vital component in the development of positive coping, social and personal skills. Adolescents who bully are more likely to come from those families where such skills are lacking.

Characteristic of Victims

A series of research studies provide a clear description of typical victims (eg. Olweus, 1978; Perry, Kusal and Perry, 1988). As Olweus (1993) points out, the characteristic picture applies as much to girls as boys although there is not a significant amount of research into bullying by girls.

The most common characteristics are those of cautiousness, sensitivity, anxiety and insecurity. These victims do not provoke, tease or show aggression. The boys amongst them tend to be physically weak (Olweus, 1978). When confronted by bullies they often cry. Their self-esteem is low and they feel as negatively about themselves as others do and frequently describe themselves as stupid or ugly. They are generally lonely and unable to maintain friendships. Olweus (1978) has labelled them *passive* or *submissive* because they seek to placate rather than be aggressive in response. Olweus (1993) believes that their 'submission reaction pattern', contributes significantly to the reasons for them being bullied.

In contrast, there is a smaller group of victims who Olweus labels *provocative* victims. They have both anxious and aggressive reaction patterns. They may have poor attention control and act in such a way that they annoy other pupils who become their bullies. It is commonly the case that their overactivity and disruptive behaviour causes them to be disliked by most children in their class.

It is, however, the first group that is of most concern to this study since there is evidence that their characteristics have much to do with the relationships and interactions that they have with their parents and other family members (Olweus, 1993). This is also supported by the results of Bowers, Smith and Binney (1992).

It seems to be the case that many of the passive victims tend to be socially withdrawn children and it is their solitariness that makes them vulnerable. Such children appear to develop the traits of social withdrawal during the preschool years; in a very real sense they are victims of parental behaviours which encourage such traits. Baumrind (1967), for example, found that the parents of unhappy, socially anxious children who showed insecurity in the company of their peers were more likely to demonstrate *authoritarian* socialisation behaviour than the parents of socially adapted children. This is further born out by findings that parents who consistently use *authoritarian* management have children who are low in self-esteem and social-confidence. One study (MacDonald and Parke, 1984) found that boys described by the their teachers as hesitant and socially withdrawn tend to have fathers who are highly directive but also less physically playful and engaging than fathers of well-adapted boys. The picture of socially withdrawn girls was less clear.

Another route from infancy to social withdrawal and victim status has already been mentioned. Research over more than 30 years has demonstrated that many socially withdrawn children are *overprotected*.

This process is probably related to a form of authoritarian management in that it is both power-assertive and intrusive on normal social skills acquisition. Overprotective parents encourage their children to be dependent upon them and also restrict exploratory behaviour. In the the writer's experience, gained from observing young children, they also initiate frequent contact with their parents, particularly their mothers, and so reinforce further parental overprotective behaviour.

The Consequences of Bullying

Some of the worst effects of bullying over the life course of individual victims are revealed by the next two case studies.

Jane, aged 24, unemployed, living at home at the time of the interview

'It started when me Dad got sent to prison for thieving off the docks. I was only five but I can remember me Mam crying and all the people down our snicket shouting at us. The kids at school started shouting at me too; 'Where's your Dad, then?', 'Where do you hide his loot' and things like that. It got worse. One big boy, Stan, kept bumping into me, knocking me down, the others would run off with me things. He said 'What's your old man going to do about it?'.

'When me Dad got out he got a job down south somewhere — we never saw him again though he kept sending Christmas cards and stuff. The bullying got worse again then. Four or five kids used to gang up on me regular. The teachers did bugger all about it. They didn't like me either. And they was scared of the big kids' parents. One of them came into the toilets when the kids was ducking me in a basin full of water. She took one look and left, scared shitless she was!'

'When I got to High School it went right on. It were funny really because a lot of the new bullies didn't know anything about me — they just picked on me because the others did'.

'I got as far as the third year. Then one day all the big kids kept picking on me. They just couldn't stop it. They called me 'Whore',

'Prossy', 'Slag'. They pinned me up against the wall and pissed all over me. They wiped their snot in my hair. I didn't go back to school after that'.

'I've never had a boyfriend and I still can't go out without me Mam. I think they stole my life'.

Jane did not respond to treatment and committed suicide at the age of 25.

Paul, aged 23-years, unemployed with acute social anxiety state

'I moved to a new school in Hull when I was five, nearly six. The kids wouldn't accept me because I spoke differently to them. My mother said they were ignorant'.

'Anyway, they wouldn't leave me alone. I had to give them sweets, money, even my new shoes. My mother spoke to the teacher — she just said that I drew attention to myself because my accent was different and that was quite enough to get the local people angry'.

'She was right as well. Christ, I mean...We only came from Manchester'.

'By the time I was ten I loathed myself, I felt I was so totally worthless that I didn't deserve to have friends. So I tried hard to get on with the bullies. In fact I almost invited them to bully me — I tried to laugh about it, make a big joke out of it. They just thought I was crazy. Hell I suppose I was'.

'In the end I got sent to a special school for maladjusted kids. Just before I left to go to it, the headmaster of my junior school said that he was glad to see me go; being a born victim had made me a lot of trouble!'

'Perhaps I was by then'.

'Anyway, I didn't get bullied at my new school. I just withdrew. Now I don't know how to meet people, make friends or even pass the time of day. And I want those things as desperately as you might want to win the pools. I cry at night wanting to be one of a crowd, to be one of the boys — to have sex with a nice woman or just chat to her'.

'The trouble is it wouldn't take her 5 minutes to realise just how bloody worthless I am'.

The last two are clearly very serious examples of the outcomes of bullying, although having made that point, however, we must be careful not to simply accept all that victims may say of their problems. Bullying cannot cause what happened to the two young people described above but it is certainly associated with their plights.

The possible long term effects of bullying on both bullies and their regular victims are well documented and are now briefly examined.

Long-term direct and indirect effects of bullying

Obviously bullying of any sort causes immediate distress. People of any age who are bullied risk a continuing and all-pervasive misery, a diminution of their self-esteem and the possibility of psychosomatic illness associated with the stress. Those who bully others regularly also risk the effects of deviant social development during adolescence and early adulthood such that their capacity to form relationships may be grossly impaired, their employment prospects reduced and the probability of them becoming defendants in legal processes much increased. In one study Olweus (1993) showed clearly that teenage boys who became victims at school between 13 and 16 years of age were, by the age of 23, more likely to show serious depressive tendencies and to have very poor self-esteem. As most were not continuing to experience victimisation at this age, it is clear that these effects are the long-lasting sequel to their victim status. Not surprisingly there has been a significant amount of research (eg, Turkel and Eth, 1990) that demonstrates that pupils who are bullied have significant problems of concentration and so find it hard to learn or solve problems effectively. Sharp and Thompson (1992) showed, from a sample size of 723 secondary-aged pupils, of whom 40 per cent claimed to have been bullied during a particular school year, that 20 per cent of these pupils said they would truant to avoid being bullied; 29 per cent claimed they found it difficult to concentrate on school work, 22 per cent experienced feelings of physical illness after being bullied and 20 per cent claimed to have sleeping difficulties.

Quite apart from the well documented association of suicide amongst teenagers who are regularly bullied there is also evidence of an indirect nature which demonstrates that victims experience continued low self-esteem and feelings of poor self-worth to such an extent that their later close relationships are not adequately based on trust and intimacy and that this can pervade the formation of close relationships with the opposite sex (Gilmartin, 1987).

Adolescents caught up in regular bullying often need help to modify their behaviour. Sometimes when they are involved with a gang of peers, they bully only as a result of peer pressure. Other adolescents, however, take part in victimisation much more actively and indeed some researchers believe that it is almost an essential part of their relationships. Typically these adolescents view the world as a tough and uncompromising place where only the strong survive; such adolescents typically interpret the actions of others as aggressive or provocative and so misread social cues provided by individuals who subsequently become their victims. Thus Bolton and Underwood (1992) showed that 44 per cent of bullies felt that they picked on victims because the victims were provocative. Conversely only 12 per cent of non-involved individuals thought this was the case.

The abuse of power

Given the research evidence and the experiences of victims we must acknowledge that bullying is the aggressive systematic abuse of power. Social relationships will always have a power aspect to them; this can result from physical size, the ability of an intelligent person to dominate a person of lesser intelligence, force of personality or sheer brute strength. There will always be opportunities for power relationships to become abusive. How we define abuse in this context is highly dependent upon social and cultural factors and it is inevitable that the victims will define it very differently to those who have power to wield. It does seem to be an inescapable part of the human condition that power relationships will at some point become abused.

This seemingly inevitable trait of power abuse opens up virtually all contexts of human activity to the sordid and negative influences of bullying. It is only by examining the attitudes that people of all ages hold towards bullying, and in particular to bullies and victims, that we can begin to understand why our power can be so readily used.

Attitudes towards bullies and victims

The common attitude towards victims is that they are provocative. It has obvious links to the general attitudes held by children and young people towards victims. The study of pro-victim attitudes has become an important part of research into bullying.

Whilst many young people express negative attitudes towards bullying (Boulton and Underwood, 1992) attitude variation is to be expected. Sex and age effects have been well recorded. Thus Hoffman (1977) claims that females are generally more empathetic than males, acknowledging both their own emotions and those of others. More specifically, females are generally found to be more sympathetic than males to the victims of aggression (Frodi, Macauley and Thore, 1977) and other research (Randall and Donohue, 1993) shows that this effect sharpens as age increases; with boys particularly becoming less supportive of victims. This finding is mirrored in Rigby and Slee's (1991) own findings which show a trend towards reducing sympathy as age increases. One possible explanation has already been touched upon; namely, the effect of 'tough' male-dominated cultures but another is also possible; namely, the general finding that boys are more likely to be bullied than girls. Boys may, therefore, be more concerned about their own status as victims and have less emotional 'time' to spare other victims. Many of Askew's (1989) findings would tend to support this. One observation from her study in secondary schools reveals that point particularly cogently. One of her young informants told her 'You always feel you have to be careful. You always feel you might be next'.

In addition, Social Learning Theory predicts that there will be an imitation effect whereby aggressive behaviour will be transmitted through the processes of modelling (eg, Bandura, Ross and Ross, 1961). Again one quote provided by Askew provides a degree of support for this belief; 'You think, 'Oh well, better him than me' and you just join in'.

Turning our attention back to Rigby and Slee's findings, we must note that they found younger children are more likely to be pro-victims than older ones and girls are more pro-victims than boys. In addition, the younger children report more bullying than older ones and there was a large majority of children of all ages who oppose bullying and support victims.

The findings of Rigby and Slee (1991) were obtained from an area where the adolescent school bullying rates are on par with other large surveys from other countries. There is evidence that attitudes towards bullying are different in areas of higher risk. For example, Randall (1994) demonstrated a significantly different profile of pro-victim attitudes present in children in a high risk bullying area then those found by Rigby and Slee. Both studies made use of the questionnaire devised by Rigby and Slee which consisted of twenty items that tap attitudes towards victims. Half these items were positively orientated (eg 'weak kids need help'), and half were negative orientated (eg 'nobody likes a wimp'). Three response categories were provided for each item: agree, unsure and disagree.

After factor analysis both sets of results showed that the majority of young people are opposed to bullying. They see it as undesirable and believe that it should be stopped. In that finding there is a strong degree of correspondence between both studies; there were, however, substantive differences.

First, the strongest factor from the high risk area study was a large anti-bullying factor whereas that of the Rigby and Slee study from an area with an average frequency of bullying showed a strong tendency to reject victims. The implication is that the children of the high risk area are more aware of the presence of bullying and attach less importance to the characteristics of victims. The second factor from the high risk area study indicated a significant negative attitude to the characteristics of victims and was similar to the first factor identified by the Rigby and Slee study. It seems a 'macho' distaste for weakness was evident from the young people of both studies. What was clear in the high risk area study was that there is some kind of separation of bullying from what happens to weak children. This is illuminated by the splitting off of behavioural components of bullying (eg name calling, being pushed around) from the factor defining the weakness of victims. There is some evidence that young people want to distance themselves from victims and believe that they get what they deserve. Does this mean that young people in a high-bullying area see some behaviour that adult observers would label as bullying as, in fact, a kind of punishment meted out by the more powerful on the undesirable?

Conversely, however, Randall's fourth factor indicates a clear wish for bullies to be punished and for victims to be defended. This is very similar to the third factor defined by Rigby and Slee and is in line with reports from other studies.

The Invasion of schools by bullying

At the start of this chapter it was stated that few schools create bullying; they may not be very good at stopping it once it arrives but in general the roots of bullying reach in to the schools from the communities they serve.

Many of the examples of bullying shown above give hints that factors outside schools are influencing the behaviour of children and young people within them. The bullying has been imported on the backs of complex social issues and domestic disagreements and, although this is not brought out by the case studies so far, there is often adult collusion in the form of the positive reinforcement of aggressive behaviour outside of the home (Randall, 1994). This case study demonstrates this clearly.

'My son, Paul, was 8 when this bullying started. To begin with it was aimed at one of his friends but as I saw it happen it was me who stopped it and complained to the head. Next thing I know Paul was getting filled in regular by three kids from the same family. The school stopped it entirely and Paul's class teacher said that one of the bullies had confessed to her that his Dad put him up to it. 'Serves them right for spragging,' he'd said'.

There is a mass of evidence that bullying occurs in just about all the institutions of the community. For example, it is well known that youth groups in deprived areas are strongly influenced by bullying (eg. Garafalo, Siegel and Laub, 1987; Van Reenan, 1992) and that frictions between neighbours are associated with bully-victim relationships in schools (Byrne, 1994). In support of the anecdotal material there is a great deal of evidence to support the view that bullying is a community problem rather than simply a school one. For example, the American psychologist Carl Jesness (1966) found that most of the vast number of delinquents he worked with during the time of his famous studies of delinquency had histories of aggression going back to their preschool years. Surveys carried out in Britain also show young violent criminals frequently have school records of physical aggression going back to infancy and an in-depth evaluations of play group entrants and three year-olds show a substantial increase to the numbers of aggressive preschool children over the last decade (McQuire and Richmond, 1986, Richman, Stevenson and Tamplin, 1985). Clearly these little children didn't learn such behaviour at school, they hadn't been there long enough. Instead they brought it with them. The following case studies illustrate just how easy it is for schools to 'import' bullying from the community outside.

Dean, an overweight boy of 14 was about to jump from the parapet of a railway bridge when he was stopped by a passing motorist. He was very distressed because of a savage game played at school each lunchtime.

Apparently he was made to stand at the centre of a ring of boys who take turns to run in to kick and punch him. Supervisory staff have witnessed this happening but, because Dean was often seen to be laughing they thought he was a willing participant in a game. Unfortunately they did not know that laughing with the bullies is a frequent defence of regular victims because they think that it will stop things from getting worse.

This 'game' had been going on for nearly two years and Dean finally was driven to a suicide attempt. On first glance the school had been negligent on doing little or nothing to stop this situation but Dean had never asked for help and the lunchtime supervisors, all untrained personnel, had not got the expertise to correctly interpret what they saw.

In fact problems existed outside of the school as well. Local people had smashed windows in his home and cut the throat of his cat. Mud was thrown at his mother's washing and excrement was posted through their letter box. All this was going on because of a feud between Dean's promiscuous mother and other women whose husbands and sons had been involved with her. These facts did not stop the mother from blaming the school for bullying. In this case the bullies were only the faithful mimics of their parents.

This study reveals how easily a neighbourhood grudge can lead to serious bullying which may mistakenly appear like a simple failure of teachers in a school.

Hannah was a small eight year old of limited ability and poor state of hygiene. She was given a very hard time at school by other pupils who resented her smell. On one occasion she was beaten by a group of girls using sticks, on another her shoes were thrown away and coat urinated on in the toilets. The pattern of bullying went on for months despite the complaints of her mother to the school.

On first sight this was a school based problem that had not been properly tackled by the staff. On investigation, however, it was found that staff acted promptly but the worse of the bullying was now going on outside of the school. The problem has not been stopped, merely re-located beyond the school gates. It transpired that the child's home was virtually under siege from a group of families living on the same estate. Many of the adults involved had records of violence including assault on their children,

Apparently Hannah's father has stolen from people in the locality and ran off before he could be caught. Hannah and her mother were left to bear the brunt of their neighbours' anger. The bullying in school was nothing more than an extension of the violence prevalent in the bullies' domestic environments and was only resolved by re-housing Anna and her mother.

Here again the school bullies were the mimics of their parents. Their behaviour stemmed from the kind of parenting they received and in some respects, therefore, they too were victims.

Bullying and Racism

One of the areas of bullying in which it is easiest to see the importation of parental negative attitudes and community sub-cultural opinion into schools is the type of bullying that is essentially racist. Ethnic minority groups make up a substantial proportion of the school population throughout much of Britain and the problems they face have been well documented (eg. Eggleston, Dunn, and Anjali, 1986). Members of ethnic minorities are extremely prone to racist bullying and, in the writer's experience, one has only to hear the nature of the taunts and threats to recognise just how significant the adult influence is on the children who practice this form of bullying. Despite the huge size of the problem there have been few studies of the incidence and process of racist bullying. In 1988 Tizzard and colleagues carried out a survey of inner London schools and their results indicate approximately one-third of pupils reported being teased because of their colour; white children reporting much less teasing than black children. Kelly and Cohn (1988) conducted another survey in three secondary schools where two-thirds of pupils reported being teased and/or bullied. Much of this was name-calling with Asian children receiving the greatest number of taunts although the figures were high for all racial groups except white.

Asian children also were found to be more frequent victims in a survey conducted by Malik (1990) whose study of 612 secondary school children showed that one-third reporting being bullied, and of these over one-third reported being bullied by pupils of a different racial background. Moran, Smith, Thompson and Whitney (1993) found that only Asian children in their survey reported name-calling on the basis of race. Qualitative responses from victims suggested that the taunts and racial statements could be very hurtful indeed. It is significant that this survey found that the Asian children did not count racist name-calling as a sufficient reason for disliking other children. This rather suggests that they accepted name-calling as a pattern of their lives in the sub-culture in which they live.

Troyna and Hatcher (1992) describe, in their book on racism in mainly white primary schools, severe racial bullying experienced by Black pupils and, more particularly, demonstrate how this behaviour is a feature of the lives of Black children well beyond the school gates. Disturbingly, they emphasise that teachers find it hard to detect this kind of bullying and they argue that even in those schools where anti-racism has been a significant part of the curriculum that many pupils who engage in racist bullying will hold anti-racist views. The implication of this is that the curriculum inputs have not been able to put 'theory into practice'. Smith and Sharpe (1994) describe how *The Heartstone Odyssey* can extend the knowledge that racism is wrong into a behavioural demonstration of this belief. Significantly, however, all schools must tackle the issue of anti-racist bullying directly and very explicitly, presenting it as an unacceptable behaviour and giving it a high priority in any anti-bullying campaign. In the writer's experience, it is necessary not only to portray the wrongness of this behaviour within the school but also to underline clearly and sharply that it is unacceptable and unnecessary to bring into school such racist attitudes as may be held by parents and other adult members of the community in which the pupils live.

Harassment and Bullying

There is an understandable reluctance for adults to consider that they have been 'bullied' by other adults in the workplace or in their neighbourhood. Despite the fact that both bullying and harassment, if there is a meaningful difference, are both instances of an intention to cause physical or psychological pain, most adults prefer to think of themselves as 'harassed' rather than 'bullied'. Adults do not like the fact that the term 'bullying' has its socio-cultural roots in the activities of children which, as we have seen, they are led to believe occurs mainly at schools. It is probably the case that many adults will not talk or their experiences of being 'bullied' for fear of being thought childish. Indeed, adult victims have told the writer that their experiences of workplace bullying have been put down to '...a mere clash of personalities' by their supervisors or as '... an inevitable aspect of stress in this hard working department'. It is no surprise, therefore, to find that many adult victims described themselves as being not only the victims of the bullies but also of those in authority to whom they have described their experiences. 'I felt to demeaned after speaking to the Personnel Manager; she made me feel as I was a little kid again spragging on someone who had been a bit nasty to me'; this statement is typical of many given by victims who have sought to use their rights under personal harassment policies of large organisations. Far from being helped, they have found that they are an embarrassment and frequently see themselves side-tracked into other departments leaving their tormenters exactly as they were.

It is possible, however, that attempts to refer to adult bullying as 'harassment' do a great deal to disguise the ugliness of harassing behaviour. It allows a great deal of very severe intentional and harmful behaviour to be swept under a carpet by placing it alongside behaviours that are merely irritating. For example, a woman who was kicked down a flight of stairs for refusing to have sex with her line manager was not allowed to say anything worse than she had been 'harassed' by him. In the same department, at approximately the same time, another woman also complained of harassment because she was not allowed the summer holiday periods that she wanted. Clearly the differences between these two sets of behaviour are extreme and it is generally better to denote the intention to cause pain as bullying in order to highlight the severity of its potential effects on victims. It is interesting to speculate perhaps, whether the woman of the first case description in this section would prefer to describe herself as 'harassed' or as 'bullied'.

Conclusions

This chapter began with an examination of bullying in terms of what it is and who does it to whom. In discussing these issues it becomes obvious that the roots of bullying lie in the community rather than in its institutions such as schools; this is particulalry true of racist bullying and is probably a factor in respect of gender discrimination. It is not schools that create bullying but the characteristics and behaviour of parents and other adults that promulgate the attitudes of children and young people which underpin this behaviour. These attitudes span the generations and result in a cyclic problem of inter-generational aggression for affected communities. The next chapter examines the parenting and bahaviour management styles that lead to this.

CHAPTER 2

The development of early aggression

The last chapter described the mechanisms through which bullying become imported into schools. It described how many of these bullies have problems other than those of simple aggression that impair their relationships and adjustment. The next stage is to consider why this should be and the responsibilities that their primary caretakers have within the process, from there we can see clearly why a community focus is best placed to tackle bullying in a particular area.

In order to move on we must first review the means by which aggression develops normally within the pre-school years and how it is generally modified into adapted assertiveness around the time of school entry. From the understanding of normal development we can then consider how maladaptive adult influences can contribute to a heightened level of aggressive activity in school and throughout the community.

Aggression: Where it comes from and how children learn to control it

We know that aggression develops in stages and that developmental factors also exist to modify each stage. The following shows the progression between birth and five years of age.

Psychologists have had a huge interest in the development and regulation of aggression that has spanned many species and has particularly involved in-depth research into hostility during adolescence and adulthood. Despite this there has really been very little by way of an examination of aggression developing during the pre-school years. In part this is due to a major interest in understanding instead how pro-social behaviour develops and how young children become socially competent (eg, Parke and Slaby, 1983). Nonetheless some researchers have analysed the early stages in the development of aggression. For example, Parens (1979) studied aggressive behaviour of infants up to two years of age and Szegal (1985) up to four years of age. This author and others have identified stages during the pre-school years during which aggression increases and other stages or periods when it shows a decrease. In general the decrease of aggression is characterised by the young child's increasing ability to inhibit emotional behaviours and I will say more of this later.

Birth to One Year

The first year of life is not one that most people would associate with either the development of aggression or, indeed, the growing ability of an infant to regulate it. Yet the observations of some researchers indicate that this is exactly what happens.

We know, for example, that anger can be produced in the new born (eg, Campos, Barrett, Lamb, Goldsmith and Steinberg, 1983). It would be a mistake, however, to believe that this anger was necessarily a forerunner of whatever emotions are associated with aggression. We must be very careful to think clearly about what aggression is and for the remainder of this chapter, we will use the definition provided by Edgecumbe and Sandler (1974) whereby an aggressive intention exists only "... when some representation and self, object and aggressive aim could exist in the mind of the child'. Most writers (eg, Harding, 1983, Kagan, 1974) demonstrate that the age at which intentional behaviour develops is somewhere between four and ten months.

The observational studies of Szegal (1985) show that the first displays of aggression generally occur between seven and twelve months and they are reported as occurring typically in response to physically painful stimuli or discomfort, experiences of tension or frustration and at times when the infant demands attention. Parens (1979) believed, however, that aggression, in terms of intentional behaviour, occurs as young as five months in association with the infant's developing sense of individuality as separate from the primary caregiver (usually the mother).

It would seem therefore that there is general agreement that aggressive behaviour, as distinct from anger, appears as intentional behaviour during the second half of the child's first year of life.

Modification of aggression occurs because of the development of a wide ranging set of skills that psychologists refer to as Affect Regulation. This can be defined as a capacity to '... redirect, control, modulate, modify and bring about, adaptive functioning in emotionally arousing situations'(Cicchetti, Ganiban and Barnett, 1990, p 1). Put simply this means that children develop the skills for behaving sensibly even in situations that are tense, emotional and likely to lead to aggression or other undesirable behaviours. Clearly, many aggressive young children do not develop these skills and their behaviour becomes excessive as a consequence.

Even during the first year of life it is possible to observe the beginnings of this regulation of aggression. It begins with the infant learning, during its first three months of life, how to regulate its own physiological mechanisms and thus keep itself more comfortable, within limits, independently of the external environment. Since much of the infant's anger at this time is associated with physical discomfort, this development leads to a concomitant reduction in the expression of anger that may be directed against the principle caretaker. Cicchetti, Ganiban and Barnett (1990) refer to the capacity for 'haemostatic regulation'. This is the internal stability achieved through the infant's stabilisation of its rhythms of eating, elimination and the sleep/wake cycle. In short a more comfortable baby equates with a less aggressive one.

During the period from three months to the end of the first year the infant's capacity and desire for social interaction increases greatly. With this comes the satisfaction of increasing competence in relating to the world. Thus, the infant develops satisfaction out of producing regular effects from certain behaviours; knocking a rattle creates a distinctive sound, shaking the edge of its crib produces a familiar vibration, and so on. These interactions and experiences allow the infant to become less dependent on the principle caretaker for 'entertainments'.

Between nine and twelve months another critical development occurs. The infant becomes able to organise affect, cognition and behavioural expression in relation to the primary caregiver. We understand the combination of these factors as the attachment relationship which comes to fulfil an increasingly complex and valuable function for the developing child. Clearly the quality of interactions with the principle caretaker, usually the mother, are of critical importance during this period and the satisfactions derived by the infant do much to increase the rate at which aggression is regulated. The infant is therefore more able to tolerate tensions and stresses without the need to respond aggressively.

This attachment relationship is fragile; a short set of aversive experiences can damage it irrevocably and the infant is likely, therefore, to be less able to move away from aggressive behaviours as a means of achieving greater comfort or entertainment.

Age one to two years

As far back as 1931, Goodenough demonstrated a rapid increase in the frequency of aggression from about eighteen months to two years. In more recent times Szegal (1985) has been able to define this pattern quite precisely. The most likely explanation for this increase is that the infant, having been used to all his or her needs being met instantly, cannot tolerate any limitations imposed by the caretaker. Parens (1979) believed that the infant cannot remember that the caretaker who makes the refusal and causes such intense frustration is also the same person who is associated with the gratification of needs and deep sustaining pleasure. It is probable that this inability to recognise the caretaker in both roles (and so use the memory of the 'good' caretaker to inhibit aggression) continues for several months into the third year of life and is at the root of the characteristic temper tantrums that give rise to the 'terrible twos'. Other researchers (eg, Mahler, Pine, and Bergmann, 1975) feel that this increase of aggression is also a result of the infant struggling towards independence and using aggressive behaviour as a means of doing so. It is noteworthy that many infants, during this time, are apt to say 'No' quite fiercely when caretakers approach them with a view to changing their activity.

Lastly we must mention the outcome of the huge number of studies that have observed infants of this age within creche and nursery settings. It is noteworthy that 'possessiveness' or the desire to acquire objects such as toys is most frequently associated with outbreaks of aggressive behaviour (eg, Szegal, 1985). Many social difficulties with peers are seen to have their roots in behaviour of this sort.

Although the 'terrible twos' may indeed be highly aggressive little individuals, it is also true to say that this is a period when a great deal of pro-social behaviour is learned. This behaviour, as we shall see, has much to do with the regulation of aggression. Typically, by the end of their second year, most children have become capable of showing and understanding a full range of human emotions. This range includes obvious emotions such as anger caused by jealousy, and sympathy as a response to pain but also more subtle emotional expressions as well. Some researchers (eg, Dunn, 1992) have been able to demonstrate that the subtle range of emotional expression enables children as young as eighteen months to know how to get each other into trouble within the home setting. The biggest single source of affect regulation for this age comes with the development of representation, language and symbolic play, all of which have an enormous influence.

Symbolic capacities, which include language and pretend play, are vital to the further development of the monitoring, modifying and regulating of the behaviour associated with emotional expression (Emde, 1985). Play and language also become much more complex and useful to the child who uses them increasingly to reduce tension and anxiety throughout the second and third years of life. The ability to express oneself verbally or through the medium of play clearly reduces aggression by alleviating the distress that often is associated with it. In addition the child is more able to use the representation of happy times and pleasant experiences during the absence of the primary caretaker; this also reduces tension and therefore diminishes the likelihood of aggressive responses from the child. Finally we note that children are more able, during this period, to use simple negotiation strategies instead of aggression (eg, Cicchetti, Cummings, Greenberg and Marvin, 1990).

Another important regulator of aggression is the child's increasing ability to be able to cope with the inhibition of his or her behaviour by the imposition of limits or rules set by adults. This can go further, in the sense that even children as young as eighteen months (Vaughn, Koop and Krakow, 1984) will limit their behaviour according to rules even when the primary caretaker is not present. Power and Chapieski (1986) found that two year olds were capable, about 45 per cent of the time, to maintain behaviour within set limits even when the primary caretaker was not present.

Finally, we must mention a most important development during this period. That is the development of an empathetic response to the stress of others. Some authors (eg, Eisenberg and Mussen, 1989) have described a sympathetic behavioural response to the distress of others from children as young as eighteen months. This development comes hand in hand with early pro-social behaviour and indicates that the child now accepts that he or she lives in a world inhabited by others who are also important and have feelings. This is a vital inhibitor of the frequency of a young child's aggressive behaviour.

Age two to three years

This is an interesting period because although it is characterised by a marked increased in the frequency of aggressive outbursts the nature of these outbursts changes quite considerably. The increase continues until about two and a half years and then gradually decreases. The child's verbal aggression expands in type and content but behaviours such as biting, hair-pulling, deliberately aiming and throwing objects, hitting, kicking and pushing are much reduced (Cicchetti, Cummings, et al, 1990, Stern, 1985). Several researchers believe that children as young as two and a half years of age can express their aggression verbally and also justify it in a rudimentary way (eg, Miller and Sperry, 1987). Much of this verbal aggression is directed against the routines of the day and the desire of the primary caretaker to exert authority when necessary.

This welcome change from physical to verbal aggression is tempered by the observation (Fagot and Hagan, 1985) that instances of physical aggression now last longer than they used to.

The regulation of all forms of aggression also improves dramatically during this period. Language and the ability to play alongside other children without territorial incidents have become much more refined and opportunities for hostility and anger are thereby diminished. Well regulated children are now able to talk about their feelings and this in turn facilitates their control over the non-verbal expression of strong emotions (Bretherton, Fritz, Zahn-Waxler and Ridgeway, 1986).

Age three to five years

As we have already noted there is a marked drop off in physical aggression before three years of age. At approximately the same time there is a significant increase in the amount of time children spend in social interactions without physical fighting. Anger is expressed but it is usually done so verbally or with the use of demonstrative body language. Such 'squabbles' generally occur over possession (Ramsey, 1987). Also at this time children start the complex process of internalising the rules and standards given to them by their families and they identify with the people who have provided those rules and standards. The modelling of social behaviour by the child's caretakers is very important during this time and, with it, comes the slow development of conscience that enables children to delay the gratification of impulses (Freud, 1968). This frees them from reliance on controls provided by others or other forms of control that are external to them. Their capacity for empathy develops and gradually they are able to accept that other people have a perspective that is different from their own (eg, Marcus, Roke and Bruner, 1985). As Campbell (1990) states they develop a sense of personal responsibility that goes along with a desire to please. These, combined also with an urge to succeed, become the tools for successful early social adjustment at school and the foundations for satisfactory academic achievement.

Nurturing successful development

As we can see from the evidence above the inhibition of aggression and the development of pro-social behaviour is dependent upon a combination of biological maturation and the nature of the environment as offered primarily by the child's caregivers. If we make the assumption that the child's biological maturation is enabled by good nutrition, adequate housing and other factors leading to good health then we can turn our attention to the environment offered by the child's caregivers. It is upon these that the complex development of vital components of personality such as empathy and self-inhibition are particularly dependent (Kopp, 1982). It would seem from our own research and studies reported previously (eg, McQuire and Richman, 1986) that the numbers of very aggressive pre-school children are growing. It would also seem clear that many of these are seriously conduct-disordered and their later emergence in school as bullies is hardly surprising. We may conclude from this that many of these children are not receiving, despite adequate biological maturation, the kind of interactions they need from their parent that encourage the inhibition of later aggression.

Inhibiting aggression

Although there is no definitive style of interaction that will always be successful for all children in bringing about the inhibition of aggression, there are nevertheless a number of important principles that are vital to the process. A brief review of these is given here:

1. Immediately from birth, the earliest contacts between the primary caregiver, usually the mother, and the infant are vital because they must provide a high level of sensitive response to the infant's needs and be governed by a high level of awareness concerning his or her signals concerning need. If these contacts are satisfactory then physiological regulation for the infant will be established. Moreover, the patterns of contact and interaction begin to be formed that later become the foundation for social relationships and styles of interacting with other people (Tronick, 1989).

2   A happy emotional tone based on loving affection during early and subsequent contacts between infants, young children and their caregivers is known to be crucial for emotional develop and the regulation of behaviour (Tronick, 1989).

Many researchers have shown that not only do infants and young children imitate or mirror their caregivers' emotional behaviour, they also depend upon the facial and vocal displays during emotional expression to guide their own affective behaviour. Their understanding of the affective meaning of emotional behaviours follows soon after but is then used to guide subsequent action and behaviour (Klinnert, Campos, Sorce, Emde and Svejda, 1983). Parents who use joyful, happy and soothing interactions with infants are more able to shift unhappy or negative emotional states to more positive ones, especially when anger, sadness and frustration threaten to overwhelm the infant. It is noteworthy that the memory traces that infants build up during these interactions have an impact throughout life. They arrive at such an early stage in life that they are seldom part of conscious memory but nevertheless continue to influence the affective state of the developing individual and, when faulty, are difficult to change through later therapeutic intervention (Cicchetti, Cummings, Greenberg and Marvin, 1990; Fox and Davidson, 1984).

3   The interaction of the parents and others (eg, child minders) are critical from another point of view. The infant is helped to become more able to tolerate negative or frustrating events because of the quality of these interactions and, more specifically, is encouraged to use language and pretend play in a manner which offsets many of the early causes of aggression arising from frustration. The successful parent 'allows' the child to be angry and to show strong emotion but also encourages him or her to use more symbolic modes to represent feelings. In a sense, the successful parent encourages the child to 'label' his or her feelings and so obviates the necessity to use more physical forms of aggression.

4   The successful parent also offers security as the child grows and develops independence. As the child begins to sample his or her environment through all the sensory modalities available so he or she is likely to explore beyond the immediate compass of the caretaker. During the course of such explorations events which challenge and

frighten the child will occur and then he or she will return for the security of interaction with the parent. The quality of this interaction will largely determine the nature of the child's future contact with the unknown and help to resolve it without recourse to aggression.

5　It is well known that the behaviour of primary caretakers becomes a model for the child's subsequent behaviour (Bandura, Ross and Ross 1969). Just as the caretaker could model aggression so he or she could also model empathy, negotiation, turn taking, caring, comforting and a wide variety of other pro-social behaviours. This modelling combined with the child's growing capacity for empathy ensure that, over time, the child is more likely to terminate episodes of aggression in order to avoid causing pain to other people.

6　Finally, the successful caretaker provides appropriate limits on behaviour and secures the child's attention to these by using successful behaviour management techniques. This does not mean that all caretakers are expert behaviour modifiers or are even aware of the operant learning basis to them, what it does mean is that a combination of common sense and the observation of others being successful, leads to successful strategies. Thus positive, pro-social behaviours are reinforced and excessively aggressive or other undesirable behaviours are sanctioned. Once the caretaker has evolved a set of successful strategies of this sort, he or she is then highly likely to use them consistently and the child is thus able, over time, to internalise the limits that are set. These ultimately evolve into an understanding and acceptance of the demands of society.

When things go wrong

The last section shows the considerable responsibility the parents or other primary caretakers have for the child's growing ability to inhibit aggression. If all goes well the parents will have created exactly the right kind of environment and style of interaction which will enable their child to develop into a social human able to take a normal place in society. It is clear, however, that the growing numbers of children of pre-school age and school entrants with severe aggressive disorders who subsequently become bullies, implies that the process does go wrong for many children. In this section we investigate the specific difficulties that can arise.

The beliefs held by the parents of aggressive children

Most of what we do in terms of social interaction is governed by a set of beliefs which relate to society's demands on our conduct. The nature of those beliefs will influence the ways in which parents respond to their children, particularly to their children's anti-social behaviour.

Research indicates that the mothers of aggressive children appear to hold beliefs about social development that are different from mothers whose children are not aggressive and who display normal social behaviours (Rubin and Mills, 1992). Even in an area such as making friends and sharing, the mothers of aggressive pre-school children were more likely to believe that their children would learn these skills through highly direct teaching. In other words, they were less willing than the mothers of non-aggressive children to allow their children any degree of experimentation, the opportunity to think about alternative perspectives, or to consider the consequences of various styles of interactive behaviour for themselves and for others. In general these mothers told their children how to behave and expected that the telling would be heeded (Siegel, 1982). Such strategies are often referred to by psychologists as 'low distancing' teaching styles and it is well known that they are associated with later poor performance in the development of interpersonal problem-solving skills (McGillicuddy-deLisi, 1982). A possible conclusion from this is that such parents who believe that social skills can be taught through direct instruction are more likely to have children who fail to learn the intended lessons.

Despite their belief in telling their children what they should do the mothers of aggressive pre-school children actually choose very indirect strategies or no strategies at all in order to deal with the aggression their children produce in comparison to the mothers of non-aggressive children. This is the case despite the fact that these mothers claim that their children's aggression makes them angry. Thus there is a distinct disparity between their stated belief and their actual parenting style which may be crudely described as laissez-faire. One possibly explanation for this is that the mothers are themselves somewhat intimidated by their child's behaviour. In an attempt to deal with the tension this causes they may be tempted to believe that it is merely the product of a short lived phase and so use non-confrontational strategies in order to keep the peace. It is inevitable, under such circumstances that inconsistent styles of management will result and this is known to perpetuate high levels of aggression (Patterson, 1986). Sadly, the mothers of aggressive children frequently do not see themselves as having any responsibility for the development of this behaviour. Instead they are more likely to attribute it to internal or temperamental factors, even to diet or additives.

Another distressing trend concerns the tendency of the mothers of aggressive children to become less and less surprised at their children's behaviour as time goes by. They become used to it and so express less surprise and anxiety about it then the mothers of children who are not normally aggressive.

A change of management style often occurs once the child is in school. When there are reports made to the mothers of their children's aggressive behaviour they are then more likely to respond with highly punitive strategies. They continue to believe that the aggression is the product of the child's 'biology' and still do not see themselves as having had a role in the original development of the aggression and, as they become increasingly unable to control the child, so their style of management becomes yet more power-assertive and punitive. As a consequence they provide precisely the models of aggressive behaviour that will reinforce what their child does subsequently.

Parent behaviours and children's aggression

The section above describes the belief system of the mothers of aggressive pre-school and infant school age children. Naturally this belief system will do much to influence the behaviour of these parents and this is also implicated in the development of further aggression from their children.

Clearly there should be significant differences between the child-management behaviours of the parents of aggressive children and those parents whose children are not aggressive. In 1971 Baumrind suggested that parenting styles could be conceptualised on two dimensions – warmth/responsiveness and control/demandingness. The first of these dimensions concerns the affective continuum of parenting; at one end it has warmth and sensitive behaviour towards a child, at the other end it has cold or hostile behaviour. The second dimension is that of power assertion. At one end of this continuum is the frequent use of very restrictive demands, instructions and a high level of control; at the other end there is a frequent lack of supervision and low to absent control. The interaction of these two dimensions leads to a four-fold description of parenting that includes:

1   Authoritative parenting characterised by high warmth and high control,

2   Authoritarian parenting characterised by low warmth and high control,

3   Indulgent/permissive parenting characterised by high warmth and low control, and

4   Indifferent/uninvolved parenting characterised by low warmth and low control (Baumrind, 1971).

Not surprisingly these four different styles of parenting lead to very different behavioural outcomes for the children. The authoritative/ democratic parenting style is frequently associated with the development of mature pro-social behaviour and successful moral reasoning. The children tend to have fairly high self-esteem, they are socially responsible, friendly, competent and cooperative with their peers and generally happy. They also do fairly well academically (Steinberg, Lamborn, Dornbusch and Darling, 1992). Those parents who, however, provide insufficient or imbalanced responsiveness and control, those who are authoritarian, permissive or uninvolved, are likely to have children who are aggressive and socially incompetent (Lamborn, Mounts, Steinberg and Dornbusch, 1991). The following comments of this section may usefully be viewed from the perspective of Baumrind's classification.

Rejection
Parental rejection is frequently recorded as being associated with early childhood aggression. Rejecting parents are more likely to apply power-assertive strategies and punishments. The general finding is that parents who are cold and rejecting towards their children, use physical punishments and whose discipline is inconsistent are more likely to have aggressive children than other parents (eg, Conger, Conger, Elder, Lorenz, Simons and Whitbeck, 1992). Weiss, Dodge, Bates and Pettit, (1992) reported that harsh parental discipline was a good predictor of child aggression in school.

The way in which parental hostility and rejection results in childhood aggression is not difficult to understand. Firstly, such a style creates a family environment that elicits frustration amongst its members. Frustration often results in feelings of anger and hostility. These feelings, if left unresolved, are likely to produce hostile and aggressive interchanges in parents and their children. Secondly, parental rejection and punishment serve as distinctive models of hostility and the inappropriate use of force (Bandura, 1971). Finally, it is also probable that parental rejection constitutes a basis for children to develop an 'internal working model' of themselves as unworthy and of the social world they inhabit as untrust-worthy and hostile (Bowlby, 1973). Such negative perspectives and feelings could easily contribute to a child's lack of empathy for others in social interactions and to the development of an increasingly refined hostile behavioural repertoire which is likely to include bullying.

Interestingly we must take note that the parents of aggressive children are not always cold and punitive; they apply their power/assertive strategies in an inconsistent manner (Parke and Slaby, 1983). Thus they may fiercely punish aggression within the home but may actually en-courage it within the peer group outside of the home. Some researchers have suggested (eg, Patterson, 1982) that such parents have aspirations for their child to dominate within the peer group and will therefore reward such behaviour in school inappropriately even though they would suppress it when it occurs within the home.

It is not only parental rejection and very punitive management strategies that lead to childhood aggression. At the other extreme parental permissiveness, indulgence and general lack of supervision also correlate with increases in children's aggressive behaviour. For example, Olweus (1980) found that maternal permissiveness of aggression was the best predictor of childhood aggression. Parental neglect and lack of super-vision of children are also known to be related to truancy, precocious sexuality, drinking problems and delinquency in adolescence and adult-hood (Lamborn, Mounts, Steinberg and Dornbusch 1991).

What if the parents were to alter their ways? Would the assumption of normal parenting styles and more common sense strategies of manage-ment lead to a reduction in the aggression of children? The answer is that it may not. The evidence is that although parenting styles are the best predictors of early childhood aggression the best predictor for later ag-gression in adolescence and early adulthood is the continuing presence of childhood aggression (eg, Hofferman, 1977). This suggests that poor parental behaviour (either rejecting and punitive or uncaring and neglect-ful) help to establish a pattern of childhood aggression which becomes the foundation for the development of poorly controlled, aggressive behaviour in later life.

What factors influence the interaction parents have with their children?

The section above has shown that many aggressive children have parents who are rejecting, neglectful, sometimes over protecting, and who use inconsistent management strategies frequently combined with excessively harsh discipline. What causes these parents to respond to their children in this way? Is it that they are all simply incompetent? Unfortunately for many that answer is the simple truth but it is by no means the whole story. There is a wide range of influences that contribute to negative feelings about child rearing that many parents have and which cause them to respond in ways which contribute to their child's later maladjustment.

It is well known, for example, that the characteristics of children are associated with the ways in which parents respond so we have something of a 'chicken and the egg' situation. Parents respond differently to children who are perceived to be 'easy' 'wary' and 'difficult'(eg, Lytton, 1990). In addition, many researchers conclude that parenting emotions, beliefs, cognitions and behaviours must be viewed within a wide spectrum of background variables that include family resources, negative and positive life experiences, the quality of the relationship between the parents and the general availability of a support network to the parent (eg, Cox, Owen, Lewis and Henderson, 1989). The following paragraphs examine some of the effects of these background variables, all of which are associated with one form of stress or another.

Stress and parenting

In recent years many researchers have attempted to determine how the experience of stress and the lack of social support can conspire to reduce the effectiveness of parenting. For example, economic stress, brought on by poverty or the misapplication of financial resources causes feelings of frustration, helplessness and anger that are often translated into poor child rearing styles. Stressful financial situations are good predictors of negativism and inconsistency towards children by their parents (eg, Weiss, *et al*, 1992). Parents who are in trouble financially tend generally to be more moody, irritable and have a lower flash point for anger than parents who have fewer financial problems. They are also less child-centred, less involved with their children's activities and are generally not as nurturant and consistent with their children than those parents who are financial secure (eg, Patterson, 1986). It is these parenting behaviours that are closely associated with the development of poor social skills in children and a weakened inhibition of aggression. Many researchers report a strong positive association between economic stress and children's poorly inhibited social behaviour, particularly aggression (eg, Dooley and Catalano, 1988; Windle, 1992).

Marital conflict or conflict between parents is also another stressor that predicts the parenting behaviour associated with child maladjustment. Discord between partners and general dissatisfaction with their relationship predicts negative attitudes to child rearing and is also associated with unresponsive parenting behaviours (eg, Jouriles, Murphy, Farris, Smith, Richters and Waters, 1991). These parenting cognitions and behaviour are, of course, strongly associated with aggression in childhood. Hostility between the parents, perhaps leading to marital violence, also affects children directly by providing them with exactly the models of aggressive behaviour that are known to reinforce aggression outside of the home. Jouriles *et al* (1991) found that child aggression is predicted by expressed hostility between the parents and it is noteworthy that this kind of marital conflict is more predictive of child aggression in boys than in girls (Block, Block and Morrison, 1981).

Another common family-based stressor is parental psychopathology. Maternal deprivation, for example, is sometimes found to be at the heart of lack of parental involvement and responsivity to children and is also known to reduce spontaneity for fun and general emotional support to children (eg, Downey and Coyne, 1990). As depression is often associated with maternal feelings of hopelessness and helplessness it is not surprising to find these effects. Depression in fathers can also produce poor parenting responses and, in fact, depression in any family member is likely to lead to less cohesion and emotional expression within the family group. It is the case, however, that parental depression does not just reduce positive interactions between parents and child. When the depressed parent does decide to take control of their life again it is often found that they do so by becoming extremely authoritative with their children. The authoritarian pattern of child rearing is often inconsistent and models the kind of aggression that children should be learning to inhibit.

We must also consider the issue of social support. One study by Jennings, Stagg and Pallay (1988) demonstrated that mothers who were more satisfied with their personal social support networks were more likely to praise their children and less likely to adopt authoritarian styles of behaviour management.

Some parental influences act on the child's development of aggression through biological mechanisms. Thus poor nutrition is implicated with developmental delay that may result in an extended period of aggressive behaviour before the regulators are fully in place. In addition there is evidence that the growing incidents of substance abuse by mothers during pregnancy (Lipsitt, 1990), and the survival of very small premature infants with serious medical and congenital defects frequently result in neurological damage (Als, 1986) and these may also be associated with aggressive conduct disorders.

Contributing to parental stress and also directly implicated with conduct problems are neurological impairments involving convulsive and memory disorders (Brennan, Mednick and Kandel, 1991) and maturation lag in the development of the Central Nervous System (Monroe, 1974) – all of which are found more frequently in aggressive children particularly if their aggression is characterised by sudden and quite explosive physical activity.

Finally a whole range of other stressful variables are known to be associated with aggression during the school years. These includes low IQ, learning difficulties and generally poor academic achievement (Lipsitt, Buka and Lipsitt, 1990).

The pathway to aggression and bullying

The variation between bullies is very great but whatever else they may be they are all aggressive children. Some may be cunning and devious in the way they present themselves as bullies and have highly complex strategies available to them that prevent detection. Others may be obvious and forever in trouble with authority figures like teachers. The sad fact that their aggression probably has its roots in their pre-school years in not something that can be dealt with at the time that they hold their terrified victims in the palms of their hands, yet we must recognise that the only satisfactory response to bullying must include work with parents of very young children in order to ensure, in high risk areas, that the cycle of aggression can be broken and the behaviour of bullying prevented before it is established. In this section we summarise what has gone before in this chapter and present the pathways to bullying that must be understood before they can be modified.

As we have seen there are many pathways to the development of aggression and these reflect the contribution of genetic, neurological, biological, psychological and sociological forces. Significant numbers of children are likely to develop early problems of aggression through environmental risk, others will do so because of their physical or neurological vulnerability and a handful are at risk from both sources. By the time their problems come to the attention of professionals such as health visitors or social workers their original difficulties are often masked behind a self-perpetuating cycle of aggressive behaviour followed by parental rejection followed by more acting-out aggression. The cycle may be firmly established and hard to break.

During the course of my community research the developmental histories of many of the worst bullies show that their earliest and subsequent interactions with their parents were of critical importance.

In most cases these interactions were unsatisfactory, inconsistent and gave neither child nor parent any sense of satisfaction. In the high risk area of the community project we noted that many of the parents of bullies themselves had unsatisfactory experiences of parenting when they were children. They forged their own parenting styles from the same power-assertive strategies that their own parents used and, often without close emotional social supports or other forms of advice, they maintained these strategies despite the obvious fact that they had little or no satisfactory impact on their children's behaviour.

In addition these bullies as infants brought their own temperamental stressors to the parent-child interactions. Their parents described them as overactive, whinging, temperamental, hard to please, often crying, with poor sleep patterns and faddy and inconsistent tastes in food. Their parents used words like 'irritable', 'angry'and 'complaining' about them. There were not to know that their infants were not responsible for these traits; they were simply the victims of their biochemical, neurological and temperamental make-up.

The writer's interviews with the parents of these bullies shows that there was never a 'goodness of fit' between them and their children. Days of peace and quiet were often interrupted by weeks of hostile, bickering and unsatisfactory behaviours. By two years of age the child had firmly established sets of behaviours designed to reduce their anxiety and tension which included long screaming or crying, bitting, kicking, tantrumming and over activity in social settings. These findings are not unlike those of other researchers, notably Sroufe (1988). The parents' response to such behaviour represents the beginnings of a circular tragedy because, as the parents become more rejecting and assertive in discipline so their children respond by even greater aggression.

Conclusions

It is not surprising that the aggressive child soon develops a sense of him or herself as 'bad', and as a result of this faulty self construct, begins to misread the social cues from others to, in a sense, always suspect the worse (Dodge and Frame, 1982). A cycle of rejection is thus established away from the home as well, in school particularly in respect of teachers and peers. Such a child is very much at risk of social and educational failure and will find few satisfactions within the complex social environment of school. Some form of conduct disorder is highly likely and if bullying brings a degree of satisfaction, perhaps from the approbation of a few hangers-on, then it becomes a probable persistent response. The child will continue to act-out his or her 'bad' self. At this point the pathway is complete, the child becomes the aggressive adolescent, the aggressive adolescent becomes the aggressive young adult – each phase in his or her development looking out at the world with increasing suspicion of the motivations of others and satisfaction achieved only through dominating those who are vulnerable or susceptible. The bully is born.

CHAPTER 3

The strategy

The previous chapters have dealt with the nature and origins of the aggressive activities we refer to as bullying. Successful intervention that will stand the test of time must address these origins in the catchment communities of schools as vigorously as the problems inside the schools themselves.

This chapter provides an overview of a successful and flexible strategy that is primarily based in the community but also enables effective within-school policies and procedures to be established.

Why Bother?

If you have obtained this book you will already have your reasons for bothering about bullying. If, however, you now have to convince others that collectively you must do something about it, be they teachers, parents, community workers, health visitors, social workers or local government officers then you need to have good answers to this question 'Why bother?'

Unfortunately many people have attitudes to bullying that are far from helpful and they need convincing about the reasons why bullying should be tackled at all. For example, infant teachers are able to identify aggressive children in their classes but are unused to the idea that such children may later develop into bullies (e.g. Chazan, 1989). As a result specific incidents of aggression may be tackled without reference to the characteristics of the 'victims'. Consequently the need of many victims to alter their own behaviour in some way may not be noticed and so go unmet, thereby making such children more likely to become victims in the future.

Other teachers, or so surveys have shown,(e.g. Stephenson and Smith, 1987), hold attitudes to bullying that almost guarantee its development. Some subscribe to the 'school of hard knocks' philosophy which concludes that children are toughened up by bullying and so better prepared for the tribulations that life will provide during adulthood. Many parents feel the same way and, in the writer's experience, this common view is held by many working in the community as well (eg. social workers, youth leaders, probation officers).

Many other teachers mistakenly believe that the only bullying going on is only that which they are aware of and are doing something about already. In fact the writer's own survey show that there is far more of this behaviour on-going at any particular time than teachers or parents are aware of.

All of these are beliefs are totally mistaken and misinformed.

Firstly, bullying does nothing to help children withstand misfortune – at best it simply teaches avoidance behaviour: at worst it leaves permanent emotional if not physical scars; neither does it fulfil any developmental process essential to children's social and emotional growth – quite the reverse, it can stunt maturity by robbing victims of the confidence and opportunities to develop normally through social exploration; finally for every one incident that a teacher knows about there will be at least another ten undisclosed (Randall, 1995).

Another popular adult-based myth is one which says 'to stop a bully is to make life worse for the victim later on'. In other words people who subscribe to this theory believe that if bullies are punished they are likely simply to bide their time and then repay the victim doubly when there is no one around to protect them. There is no general evidence, however, that adult intervention produces worse or more secretive bullying of the same victims. In fact, to turn a blind-eye may result in unwitting adult collusion with the bullies and consequent reinforcement of their behaviour (Randall, 1991).

To summarise what is known of the outcomes of long term bullying;

Outcomes for bullies

*   poor long term peer relationships,
*   aggressive behaviour perpetuated into adulthood,
*   faulty impression of own importance,

- lack of trust in other people,
- oppressive attitudes to minority groups, gender discrimination, etc.,
- poorer than normal response to training/employment,
- poor marital/partner relationships,
- perpetuating aggressive behaviour in own children because of aggressive models of behaviour.

Outcomes for victims

- long term unhappiness/misery,
- much increased probability of depression or emotional disorder,
- low self-esteem and feelings of low self-worth,
- reduced social skills,
- failure to develop effective assertiveness,
- poor long term social relationships,
- truancy,
- poor concentration,
- sleeping difficulties / appetite disorders.

Given this constellation of direct and insidious problems it is obviously well worth the efforts of all members of the community to put an end to the problems caused by bullying. Such facts need to be presented clearly and powerfully, supported by case studies and, if possible, by victims and bullies themselves.

What is the Aim of a Community Approach?

The obvious aim is to stop or reduce bullying wherever it may occur in the community that is involved in the programme. There is nothing wrong with such an aim, it is perfectly logical. Yet it is a negative aim in that it does not state a positive alternative to bullying. Ideally the programme should function in such a way that bullying is not only reduced or stopped altogether but is replaced by some better, more acceptable behaviour.

There are many ways of stating such an aim but one chosen for the large community projects that the writer has been involved with took this as their main aim:

To eradicate bullying and to promote an environment in which it cannot thrive and which strives to improve peer relationships throughout the community.

Although this book is not about these projects this aim is useful in illustrating both the positive and negative aspects of work to counter bullying.

One of the virtues of such an aim is that it covers the 'direct' and 'indirect' bullying that occurs. Olweus (1993) shows that pupils that suffer direct bullying in which they are attacked verbally, physically or in some other way, are also susceptible to an indirect form of bullying in that they are frequently excluded from their peer group (victims are not popular) and so have fewer opportunities to form friendships. He also points out that some students are not necessarily the victims of direct bullying but are nevertheless the victims of rejection and passive hostility. So an aim which directs work towards improved peer group relationships will do much for such people in terms of greater self-confidence, social support and improved general quality of life.

What can be accomplished?

A healthy realism is needed when establishing any intervention project for bullying. As has been described bullying is rife in society and probably always has been — no single project is going to eradicate it totally. This does not mean that society should not aim to achieve precisely that; after all aims that are not met encourage greater efforts and there is always room for improvement.

In general, however, the outcomes of school focused anti-bullying programmes suggested that the following are possible (e.g. Sharp and Smith, 1994).

- the number of pupils reporting being bullied is reduced

- the number of pupils who report incidents of bullying to staff is increased

- the duration of bullying incidents with victims is reduced

- children and young people are more likely to support each other against bullying

- the number of pupils who believe that their school staff are taking action against bullying increases to a substantial majority.

With regard to the community around schools, the writer's own experiences suggest that:

- the number of people reporting being bullied in the community is reduced,

- members of the public living and/or working in the community are more likely to report bullying pupils to their schools,

- statutory agencies serving the community (e.g. social services, housing departments and the police) are more likely to take action against regular bullies,

- members of the public, particularly parents, become more aware of the 'symptoms' of bullying,

- members of the public living and/or working in the community are more likely to intervene (if only at a reporting level),

- child and adult victims are more likely to be sympathetically treated by their families, and

- bullies in the community are less likely to attract the support of a group of admirers.

In addition to these highly desirable outcomes there also seem to be peripheral benefits for schools, such as reduced vandalism, truancy and aggression in general (Roland, 1989). It is probable, in my experience that these also filter through to the environment outside of schools.

Some of these indicators can be achieved very rapidly. For example, a vigorous school implementation of policy can lead to a significant reduction in reported bullying within a few weeks but the slightest relaxation of the policy can send the rate up again just as quickly. Long term permanent benefits only come with a long period of consistent effort. To 'turn around' the traits of a hostile community will take longer still although some factions of the community will quickly gather to give invaluable support. Parents, in particular, will soon gain confidence in coming forward to help as strategies to support them lead to an effective 'team spirit'. Their reticence and nervousness will return, however, if the vigour of the programme is allowed to fade away. Patient, steady and well-coordinated effort will, however, be rewarded as the community habituates to its new responsibilities and takes ownership of them. This is not merely my own experience, community empowerment projects around the world have reported similar findings (Eg. Roberto, Van-Amburg and Orleans, 1994; Ovrebo, Ryan, Jackson and Hutchinson, 1994; Eisen, 1994).

Minimum Requirements

Anti-bullying policies are not to be attempted lightly; if the right resources, both human and material, are not in place then failure is highly probable. The material resources will be implicit to each phase of the programme but the human resources deserve a special mention at this point.

Of all the human resources required, tenacity is probably the most important. This boils down to a determination at all times to see the programme through. Anything less than utmost commitment will let down all these victims whose lives could be immeasurably improved if the tyrant's foot was removed from their necks. But beware; there is evidence (e.g. Roland, 1989) that a superficial approach to the programme may leave the frequency of bullying unchanged, or even slightly raised. Worst still, in the writer's experience, a programme that finishes after awareness of the misery of victims has been raised may actually cause an increase in bullying because these effects are actually 'advertised' to a group of potential bullies who might otherwise have remained ignorant of the power they have to abuse.

Given that commitment and tenacity are available in sufficient quantities what follows is a minimum list of resources needed to support them

- sufficient time for key personnel to devote to the programme;
- an Implementation Group of key people which reports to the Steering Group;
- a separate Monitoring and Evaluation Group able to co-opt members of the Implementation Team and which reports independently to the Steering Group;
- sufficient funding or avenues for funding to cover the programme over at least a three year period;
- full, clear and public support from the senior managers of all personnel involved in the Steering Implementation and Monitoring groups;
- access to most individuals and agencies who have significant influence in the target community;
- access to elected representatives, school governors, community leaders, and services that are associated with pre-school and school age children;

- flexibility of timetable duties to allow sufficient time to run the programme;
- a full commitment from headteachers, playgroup leaders and parent groups to the aim of reduced bullying,
- full support of the local media.

Forming the Groups

The success of the project ultimately depends upon the energy, skill and enthusiasm of the groups listed above. The Implementation Group is particularly vital because this is the 'powerhouse' of the project, the people who will organise the work on a daily basis and get it done. It will also be split into sub-groups from time to time, an Audit Group, for example, which is described in Chapter 5 and is responsible for examining the profile of bullying that occurs in the community outside of the schools.

This section makes suggestions for the formation and constitution of these groups.

The Steering Group: This group is responsible for the overall direction of the project and to ensure that it has sufficient funds to continue properly. The Steering Group should also be responsible for disciplinary matters, complaints from members of the public and public relations. The members should also represent the Project through public relations exercises and to service executives of statutory and voluntary services.

The meeting of this group should be defined within the constitutional documents and no decisions should be made unless the group is quorate (generally a third or more of members present). The minutes should be cumulative and given to public sections if public funding is assisting the project.

Members of the group should be fairly senior people who are used to managing professional activities and the budgets associated with professional services. In addition, however, it is important that members are drawn from the community to represent those people who live in it and who should benefit from the project. A useful group is therefore made up of:-

A headteacher of a comprehensive school in the community,
Headteachers of primary schools; one from each group of primaries feeding the comprehensive schools in the target community (usually no more than two),
A senior psychologist from the local school psychological services;

A manager from the health centres in the target areas,

A health visitor,

A Team Leader of the local social work teams,

A Youth Leader with management responsibility,

A Parent Governor,

A representative of the community, usually a counsellor who is Chair or Vice Chair of an important local authority committee,

A representative of the local council for voluntary services,

An employer with strong attachments to the area,

A trade union representative,

A local media editor, and

A high ranking public officer with a community brief.

The Implementation Group: As its name suggests, this group is responsible for implementing the project. Its Chairperson should sit on the Steering Group and it must report regularly to that Group.

The Implementation Group should have the power, if it is quorate, to make executive decisions and also to deal internally with complaints provided that it reports all of these. The minutes of its meetings should also be minuted on a cumulative basis and be available to public scrutiny.

Amongst its many tasks will be the strategy planning of the project, the gathering together of resources and accounting for all monies received and spent.

The constitution of the Implementation group should be identical with that of the Steering Group although it will be larger and probably less 'highpowered'. For example, although it is desirable for a headteacher to be a member of this group it is more important that teachers at the grass roots are also present, preferably those who have a lot of contact with parents.

It is also important that the health visitors in the area are well represented in this group; they have enormous good will with young parents and are frequently the first professional such members of the community turn to. Youth workers are also important because they have excellent contacts with adolescents at a time when peer group harassment is at its worst.

Finally, it is a good idea to have an experienced and local educational psychologist on the group because he or she is likely to have an intimate knowledge of the weakness of the schools in the area and will also have the skills necessary to help draw up strategies that are workable and capable of effective monitoring.

The Monitoring and Evaluation Group: This should be an entirely independent group answerable to the Steering Group. It also receives reports from the Implementation Group and has responsibility for the scientific evaluation of progress towards the objectives of the project and reporting on this progress in a business-like manner

This should only be a small group and one of its members should also be on the Steering Group so that matters of policy can be accurately relayed to it. It will need to get all the audit information at the start of the project (see next chapter) and will suggest both interim and final 'testing' of the project as it proceeds.

An educational psychologist is an ideal person to chair this small group because he or she will have the research skills to guide the other members. A psychologist is also likely to have access to the computers and software to assist in analysing results and preparing the report.

What are the Goals?

The aim given above was:

'To eradicate bullying and promote an environment in which it cannot thrive and which strives to improve peer relationships throughout the community'.

Such an aim may be worked towards from a variety of angles. We might consider these angles to be the Goals underpinning the Aim. So, for example, one goal might be to raise awareness within the community of the problem of bullying so that people can begin to think about it and what role they might have in what is going on. They might, as a result of this awareness, realise that people should intervene to stop bullying, even if that is by simply reporting it to a relevant authority. After all if victims could stop being bullied by themselves then they wouldn't be victims.

Another goal might be to link all the schools in a community by a common reporting system so that between-school bullying could be more efficiently dealt with.

A sample of goals attached to project Aims is shown as Table 3-1. These were established for a joint community project that the writer is associated with. They are general in nature and would not suit all community and school situations. The successful meeting of each of these goals goes some way towards meeting the overall aims; notice also how critical indicators of success are attached to most of the goals – these represent some sort of standard that must be attained if the goal is to be achieved successfully.

Table 3.1 Aims and goals of a joint anti-bullying project linking two communities

The aims of the joint project are listed below together with the subserving objectives and critical success indicators (CSIs) where they may be derived:

Aim 1. To establish a joint policy and code of practice between all the schools and other formal and informal institutions that serve children and young people in selected communities so that incidents of hostility/aggression can be monitored and inhibited.

1.1 To liaise with all schools, playgroups and similar facilities in the areas and provide such training as is necessary (CSI – liaison complete with four months of commencement, training complete within twelve months).

1.2 To provide packs of materials for training and awareness raising for parents (CSI – distribution complete within six months).

1.3 To assist school governors and staff to create a unified anti-bullying policy which will inform good practice in the areas, involve parents, pupils and young people and assist victims of all ages (CSI – completion within eighteen months).

1.4 To reduce the baseline frequency of bullying of children and young people by 50% over the span of the project.

Aim 2. To empower members of the specified communities to take action to stop bullying.

2.1 To engage local media in the project over its time span (CSI — at least three newspaper items, four radio and one poster campaign in each community within six months of project start date).

2.2 To work with local traders, trade union representatives, employees and employers federations to secure anti-harassment policies (CSI-commence liaison within three months).

2.3 To establish contact systems within the specified communities to promote effective 'anti-bullying' strategies.

2.4 To establish local resource centres with support and attendance from/by local politicians (CSI – within 12 months of project start date).

2.5 To secure community ownership of the local projects by 1997.

Table 3.1 Aims and goals of a joint anti-bullying project linking two communities (continued)

Aim 3. To help parents engage successfully with their preschool children in ways which will further social and educational development.

3.1 To establish parent training groups in order to promote pro-social skills amongst the preschool population of the specified communities (CSI-liaison to commence with preschool providers within four months).

3.2 To provide free parent packs and relevant materials to assist parents with early child social development.

Aim 4. To provide highly effective personal services to families or individuals within the specified communities.

4.1 To provide a high quality support, counselling and intervention service based firmly upon anti-oppressive practices to families and individuals for whom social and psychological difficulties reduce the quality of life.

4.2 To establish a supportive 'hotline' and telecounselling service.

Aim 5. To thoroughly monitor the above and provide evidence of success and/or failure and so design an effective anti-bullying modular strategy for the use of communities everywhere.

5.1 To obtain all necessary data and submit it to appropriate analysis over the period of the joint project.

5.2 To provide clear reports at all major project phases and publish these widely.

5.3 To establish all successful strategies, practices and policies within a 'portable' modular structure which can be made freely available to community representatives.

Just as the goals subserve the Aims so each goal needs one or more objectives which must be achieved in order that the goal is met adequately. So, for example, a goal about raising awareness in the community could have the following amongst its set of objectives:

Goal: To raise awareness in the community of the problems caused by bullying.

Objectives: The local free paper has carried an article about local victims of bullying.

The local radio has interviewed victims who have volunteered to tell their story.

The community leisure centre has a display stand giving information on bullying.

All school governors have received a fact sheet on bullying.

All parents have received a fact sheet on bullying.

All pupils have been to one school assembly about bullying (project provides the material).

All pupils have received a ball-point pen with the Anti-bullying logo and hotline number painted on it.

These and other objectives, once attained, all go some way to meeting the goal of awareness raising. Furthermore, these objectives can form the detail of a strategic plan for the intervention. Beside each of them the designers can insert details of timescale, resources required and responsible personnel. The next section describes how this may be efficiently accomplished;

Probably the most efficient planning technique for an anti-bullying project is the Bar Chart plan. This is sometimes known as the Gantt chart after the person credited with its invention. It is extremely useful because it can show all the major planning factors:-

- key events
- major activities
- direction of activities
- start dates
- finish dates
- resources required, and
- personnel involved.

Activities are shown as bars against a timescale, usually days and the length of each bar shows how long the activity is expected to take, when each bar starts on the chart represents the date it is supposed to start and where it ends is the predicted finish date.

A bar chart is easy to produce and gives people who are not used to planning techniques an easily understandable visual representation of the plan. Another distinct advantage is that it allows for individual activities to be broken down as finely as needs be and also charts can be super-imposed on top of each other (if acetate sheets are used) so that planners can see how different phases of the project can be run simultaneously and which activities must await the completion of other activities.

The Programme Strategy in Outline

Given Aims and Goals similar to those described above it is then possible to begin to outline the phases of the programme. These phases reflect the process required by the programme as different goals are attained and new ones come on stream. Each phase represents progress towards the Aim or Aim but is an important attainment in its own right with considerable benefits for whichever part of the community is mainly involved. What follows is a brief description of these phases. It is assumed that a suitable community has already been identified and that there is general agreement about its need.

Phase 1: Raising Awareness of Bullying

In relation to school-based programmes Olwcus (1993) believes that two general conditions must be realised. The first is that adults at the school must become aware of the extent or size of the bullying problem. They must then decide to engage themselves '...with some degree of serious-ness' in tackling that problem.

This advice is every bit as relevant to a community programme. Adults have to become aware of the size of the problem in their community and the impact that is has on victims. They will already know that bullying exists, unless they totally delude themselves, but they may choose to believe that it is a normal event which is no worse where they live than elsewhere. Awareness raising, therefore, is more than just acknowledging that some bullying is going on, it is also a matter of becoming shocked and indignant (or at least, perturbed) about its extent and its effects.

Once this level of awareness has been achieved it is relatively easy to persuade influential people that they must help to do something about it.

Table 3.2: A Partial Gantt Chart for Phase I of a Project

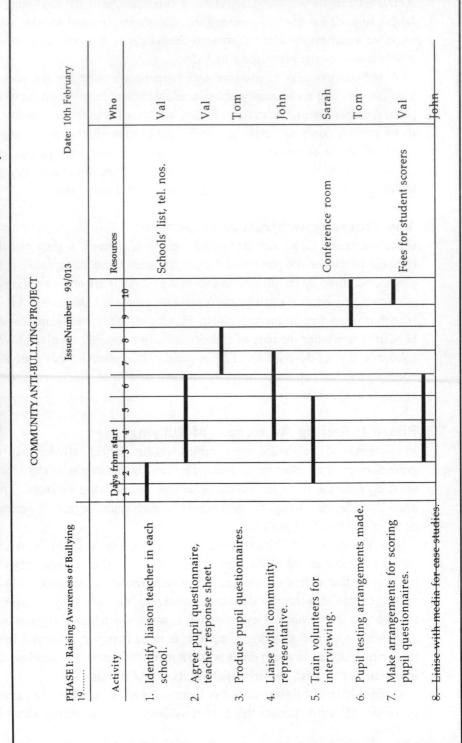

COMMUNITY ANTI-BULLYING PROJECT

PHASE I: Raising Awareness of Bullying
19.........

IssueNumber: 93/013

Date: 10th February

Activity	Days from start										Resources	Who
	1	2	3	4	5	6	7	8	9	10		
1. Identify liaison teacher in each school.											Schools' list, tel. nos.	Val
2. Agree pupil questionnaire, teacher response sheet.												Val
3. Produce pupil questionnaires.												Tom
4. Liaise with community representative.												John
5. Train volunteers for interviewing.												Sarah
6. Pupil testing arrangements made.											Conference room	Tom
7. Make arrangements for scoring pupil questionnaires.											Fees for student scorers	Val
8. Liaise with media for case studies.												John

To follow the advice given by Olweus will first involve the project staff in obtaining incidence figures from schools and community members. This will determine the size of the problem and may also yield invaluable information about the range of bullying activities within the area.

Secondly, it will be necessary to gain victim accounts of bullying and how it has affected them. This will provide information for relaying on to adults in the community about the impact of bullying locally.

Both of these are covered in detail in the next two chapters.

Phase 2: Establishing the Network

This phase is comprised of a number of stages each of which have their own complexities and need careful planning.

Stage 1. Identify the elements of the network: we have already touched on this and Chapter 6 gives further detail. Essentially what is required is a network of people and the services they represent. So, for example, a health visitor not only will bring a great deal of expertise in working with the parents of pre-school children; s/he is also able to tap into the resources of a community health trust. This could be vital when establishing a line of communication to the parents of pre-school children and the strategic placement of posters and other literature in general practitioners' surgeries and health centres.

Similarly a child protection officer from the local social services department will bring along a great deal of personal expertise about the grey areas that the programme will uncover in relation to possible child abuse. As has been shown aggressive children are very likely to have aggressive parents who use physical punishments to manage child behaviour. Since most of the cases of child physical abuse arise in the context of 'discipline' (Frude, 1992) it is likely that such issues will arise during the life time of the programme and expert advice would be invaluable. Not only that, of course, such an officer may be able to access the comparatively huge resources of a major local authority department.

Stage 2. Encourage community representatives to join the project: such representatives include those elected democratically to serve as counsellors, but also include parent governors for the schools, trustees of local charities, local employers and trade union representatives, executives of local housing trusts, police liaison officers and many others.

Each of these will have rather different motives for being involved in an anti-bullying project and it is important to discover what these are in order that the individual can be persuaded to join the network and function actively within it.

Stage 3. Engaging the local media: At this point it is relevant to introduce the concept of Community Empowerment. An anti-bullying programme that is focussed on a local community is really one of a variety of community empowerment programmes, just as anti-crime programmes such as Neighbourhood Watch are.

Community empowerment, which is discussed in detail in Chapter 6, is a process by which a defined community of people take upon themselves, with assistance, the resources and strategies needed to bring about some communal aim that is of benefit to them.

Throughout the course of a host of such programmes, some of which are reviewed later, the role of the local media has been pivotal. An anti-bullying programme deals with issues that are of great interest to media personnel and there is generally little or no difficulty in engaging their support.

Local media includes:

- Daily/evening newspapers
- Free or 'trade' newspapers
- Weekly newspapers
- Parish magazines
- Local radio

It can be helpful to have someone in a management position from the first or last of these on the Implementation Group. The (deputy) editor of a daily newspaper, for example, could ensure a regular news feed of articles and editorials that would support the project.

Given this support it is then possible to produce promotional literature for shops, public houses, health centres and other facilities which can refer to the local media sponsorship.

Phase 3: Parent Groups

By this phase it is probable that the programme is soon ready to commence. It is at this time that it should be possible to establish parent groups, particularly of pre-school children, for the work that is later to start with them. These groups can be based on existing parent groups associated with playschools, nursery school and units and mother-toddler groups. It is necessary to identify one or more parents to take part in the Implementation Group.

Phase 4: Establishing a reporting system

The purpose of establishing a reporting system is to create an environment in and around schools where bullying cannot thrive. As has been described one of the problems which prevents the successful control of bullying is that witnesses fail to do anything about it. Even the simple and anonymous reporting of bullying can do much to reduce the rate of the problem, particularly outside of schools. A simple and effective reporting system throughout the community must be established and be heavily promoted by the media. In the main the reporting system need be no more than an agreement between the headteachers of the schools in the community that members of the public may ring and report pupils of their schools who are seen to be bullying other children. Once reported the bullying pupils are then subject to the schools' disciplinary procedures. This system works well to reduce the out-of-schools bullying which may be dispersed beyond the school gates by anti-bullying measures within the school.

Phase 5: The Launch

Although much work will already have been done in order for the project to have reached this phase there is still a good point to having an official launch to mark a start date. This is an opportunity for the whole community to become aware that the project is their property and has begun to work for them.

The launch should be highly public, involve as many members of the Implementation Team as possible and definitely have the local media in attendance.

Summary

This chapter has laid out the main features of the community programme. Moving from its aims of reducing bullying and preventing it from thriving, a series of supporting goals was derived, each of which has its own set of objectives. These objectives are best met by working through the phases described above. Each of the main elements of the programme is described in the chapters which follow.

CHAPTER 4

The bully audit in the school

Introduction

The last chapter made two major points about bullying activity in the catchment schools. It is necessary to show why there is a problem of bullying and how big the problem is in terms both of frequency and impact on victims. Such details are needed to engage the concern of those who live in the community and those who serve it.

There is also a further important reason — to establish a baseline from which the progress of the project can be gauged. It is good science, as well as an ethical requirement (eg. Hudson and Macdonald,1986), to have an objective measure of the baseline in order to demonstrate that an intervention is or is not working. It is not sufficient to rely on subjective opinion that conditions may or may not be improving. Although qualitative data is invaluable when re-designing and modifying an information programme as it proceeds through its phases, the best evidence that good progress is being made is quantitative (McNiff, 1988).

The kind of information needed is obtained by using the same set of information retrieving devices throughout. There is a wide variety of methods of collecting useful data and some of these are presented overleaf.

In the context of an anti-bullying programme the data collected should show the frequency and duration of bullying events diminishing and the frequency of pupils (and adults in the community) who make reports of bullying going up. Video tape evidence should show reduced rates of

Method	Advantage	Disadvantage	Uses(s)
Filed notes	simple, on-going, personal	subjective, need interpretation need a lot of practice to do well	for specific uses, for general impressions
Audio tapes	accurate, easy to use, gives a lot of data	transcription difficult and time-consuming	for detailed evidence, diagnostic
Interviews and discussions	wide-ranging	time-consuming, needs training	for specific in-depth information
Diaries	provides personal perspectives	very subjective and hard to interpret	diagnostic triangulation of needs
Video tapes	powerful demonstration of problem areas, ideal for publicity	hard to obtain, expensive, need a lot of conents	demonstration of need, diagnostic
Questionnaires	highly specific, easy to give, cheap	need very careful design and analysis	gaining specific information/ feedback
Sociometry	easy to do, guides action	threatening to isolated individuals	analysis of social relationships
Case studies	accuracy, respresentative, ideal for publicity	time-consuming subjective	comprehensive review of problems, for publication

bullying in 'hotspot' areas and case studies should show improved positive feelings and increased self-esteem. Whatever other methods are used, a suitable set of measures should be obtained from an easy-to-use repeatable device which is valid when used with a sufficient sample size to make its estimations accurate. The most obvious instrument is a questionnaire that can be used readily by its recipients.

In recent times the questionnaires used by anti-bullying projects owe a great deal to the work of Professor Dan Olweus who was the Director of Norway's national anti-bullying campaign that took place in the 1980s. He and co-workers such as Dr. Erling Roland made extensive use of questionnaires to secure the baseline and monitoring data they needed to prove the worth of their work with schools. Since then several projects (e.g. Smith and Sharpe, 1994; Rigby and Slee, 1991) have made good use of the

Olweus questionnaire or modifications of it. The one given here also has its origins in that earlier work.

The questionnaire is not the only information seeking device that is useful to a community project. It is also necessary to have a means of gaining information on the impact bullying has on pupil victims. This requires accounts of what victims have experienced and how they felt about these experiences in order to build up a portfolio of subjective data about victimisation in the community's schools.

It is hardly surprising to find that interviews of pupils under specified conditions is a useful means of obtaining data. How these may be carried out in a credible and consistent way is also described in this chapter.

Finally, designers of anti-bullying projects need to discover where bullying activities most frequently take place. The point has already been made that bullying is an essentially secretive activity in that bullies choose their time and place in order to avoid detection. The physical environments of schools and the communities they serve often abound in suitable opportunities for the bully. These opportunities need to be exposed in order that adult supervision may be properly focussed and victims gain protection. Questionnaires and interviews are useful in detecting these bullying 'hotspots' and the design of both needs to take this into account. Each school and area around it, through which victims must travel daily, has its own bullying 'hotspots'. An old building with long corridors, isolated toilet block and deep stair wells will present very different opportunities to the bully than a single storey open plan school with landscaped grounds and detached boiler houses. Council estates with a warren of walkways present different problems from those of a leafy suburb where the pretty shrubbery makes an ideal cover for surprise attacks. Such factors need to be evaluated for their contribution to the frequency and nature of bullying in the schools and their catchment.

In addition, the questionnaire component of the survey needs to throw light on other important issues. Most experts in this area believe that it is vitally important to determine who pupils perceive as people worth telling about bullying (e.g. Olweus, 1993)). The reason for this is that they may have an already established pattern of reporting which can be improved or built upon. Also it is as valuable to learn who pupils do not tell about bullying. This may indicate which people, perhaps staff or parents, hold attitudes which involuntarily support bullying. Clearly these people need working with in particular ways to help them reverse this trend and so become more supportive of victims.

Interview data can then be used to explore why pupils perceive both the approachable and unapproachable people in the ways that they do and so more sharply focus the relevant process of the intervention programme.

A basic piece of information to be discovered from the pupils is who is perceived to actually be doing something positive about bullying and what it is that they are doing. It would be over-simplistic to believe that such responses would always be positive and therefore should be increased. On occasion an adult's response to bullies is to bully them, '...give them a taste of their own medicine'. In fact this kind of response, although supportive of victims in the short term, may simply model hostile power-assertive behaviour over less powerful individuals (Bandura, Ross and Ross, 1961). In the long term it may simply act to create more refined bullying.

From these preliminary points, it should be clear that the basic bullying questionnaire and interview structure should be tailored to meet the characteristics of the target community and its schools. There are both advantages and disadvantages to this as are now described.

Advantages

1. The structure is more likely to reflect the schools' characteristics than one that is imported from other projects.

2. Pupils and parents can be involved in the design and so, right from the start, they are given a voice and a sense of ownership. This is a valuable environment strategy.

3. Pupils respond to a structure that concerns *their* lives and their environment with greater ease than when they have to extrapolate from a more generic device to their particular situation (McNiff, 1988).

Disadvantages

1. It is easier and less time consuming to take a structure that has already been designed and proved its worth.

2. A locally produced structure needs to be tried over at least one pilot run, modified by experience and re-run before its data can be held credible.

3. The treatment of the obtained data is hard to bring into line with other surveys. Such comparisons can be important. If, for example, there is

a need to research the question 'Is our community/school different from others' then it will be necessary to use or incorporate key items from selected other surveys.

4. People who design survey instruments should not be the ones to use them or analyse the data. There may be a problem of looking for support for 'pet' theories or, the other side of this coin, challenges from others that that is what has happened.

Designing and Implementing the Survey

Questionnaire Material (Bullying frequency/severity): It is up to the designers of each community programme to decide if the advantages listed above outweigh the disadvantages. It is possible to obtain commercially available bullying survey material for schools which has been very carefully researched (e.g. Sharp and Smith, 1994). The results are valid and can be used for direct comparisons with many large projects including the superb DFE Sheffield Anti-Bullying Project recently conducted by Professor Peter Smith and his colleagues at Sheffield University. In addition there is the *Life in Schools* checklist originally designed by the senior educational psychologist, Tiny Arora, and used extensively within Wolverhampton LEA. This checklist is given at the end of this chapter with instructions for its uses. It is free of copyright but Tiny Arora should be given an anonymised copy of any results obtained and a copy of any modifications made to the checklist.

(Tiny's address for correspondence is:
Division of Education, University of Sheffield, 388 Glossop Road, Sheffield, S10 2JA.)

The writer has found this checklist to be extremely useful and, as can be seen, it does permit the calculation of two indices; the Bullying Index and the General Aggression Index, both of these can contribute to the baseline and on-going monitoring required by the project.

It is, however, possible to use an established survey questionnaire and modify it to meet particular needs for each school. The questionnaire shown below gives the minimum number of items needed to tap all of the issues descried in the introduction. It can be easily added to in order to bring out particular features which school staff would like to evaluate more fully.

INITIAL BULLYING INVENTORY PUPIL QUESTIONNAIRE

Put a tick (√) here ... if you are a boy
Put a tick (√) here ... if you are a girl

How old are you? ...

Please read each question carefully and put a tick (√) next to the answers you think are right.

1.	Do you think bullies are always	BOYS GIRLS BOYS AND GIRLS
2.	Are bullies always bigger than you?	YES NO
3.	Are bullies always older than you?	YES NO
4.	Do bullies: Hit children? Call them names? Say they will hurt them? Take things?	
5.	Have you ever been bullied / picked on?	YES NO
6.	Have you ever been bullied at this school?	YES NO
7.	How often has this happened? Once Twice More	
8.	Have you been bullied this week?	YES NO
9.	Are bullies: On their own? With friends?	

10. Where does bullying happen:
    Classroom?
    Playground?
    Toilets?
    Outside school

11. Who do you tell   TEACHERS
                                             PARENTS
                                             YOUR FRIENDS

12. If you told somebody, did it stop?   YES
                                             NO

13. Have you seen other pupils being bullied
    at this school?   YES
                                             NO

14. Did you tell anyone?   YES
                                             NO

15. FREE COMMENT ITEM

16. Have you seen bullying away from school?   YES
                                             NO

17. How often do you see it:
    Every day?
    Every week?
    Every month?
    Not often?

18. Have you been a bully?   YES
                                             NO

19. Did you bully anyone this week?   YES
                                             NO

20. Who helps you most with the bullies:
    Teachers?
    Parents?
    Your friends?
    Nobody?

The questionnaire should be given to all pupils in the school at the same time following an earlier announcement. Although the procedure for administration is not rigid, the following guidelines indicate a tried and tested strategy:

1. A teacher familiar to each class group should administer the questionnaire on a Friday afternoon (it is important that this time is chosen as some of the items ask for details of bullying or related activities that occur during the course of that week).

2. The questionnaire should be introduced by a brief class discussion about its purpose in helping to deal with bullying and what individual class members understand by the terms 'bullies', 'bullying', etc.

3. For primary classes it is generally better to talk the pupils through each item to ensure that young ones or those with poor reading skills share a common understanding.

4. It is quite legitimate to substitute the pupils' own vocabulary/idioms within items. For example, many primary age children sampled during my research made greater use of the phrase 'being picked on' for '...being bullied'. As long as the meanings are clearly shared and understood the validity of the exercise will not be significantly diminished.

5. Item 8 'Have you been bullied this week' is crucial because it supplies a timeframe. Most children from 6 onwards will be able to recall the significant events of a school week but memories frequently become blurred and distorted if the timescale is left undefined or made too long. Nevertheless it may be necessary to clarify what is meant by '...this week'.

6. Item 10 is about 'hot spots' and can be modified and extended to meet the particular geography of the school and its catchment area. It can be extremely useful to use photographs, diagrams or maps of the school buildings and important features around the school to stimulate thoughts about these potential hot spots.

7. The act of completing the questionnaire will do much to stimulate thinking about bullying and it is generally useful to hold a class 'debriefing' discussion on the subject immediately after the administration. Careful notes should be taken of any significant information that is elicited.

8. Compilation of the data should be carried out by someone other than the person who administered the questionnaire. This prevents serious accusations of 'data rigging' that might come from outside the school.

9. The data analysis needs to be no more sophisticated than the listing of simple percentages. A sample report is presented below to illustrate this, notice that it begins with a repeat of the questions that the subjects responded to in order to facilitate understanding what percentages are associated with which questions.

10. Before the data and conclusions are released for general consumption each class teacher should complete a questionnaire about their own class group. A suitable one is shown on page 66:

11. Data from the pupil's and teachers' checklist should then be transferred on to a School Summary Record. A very simple but suitable one for children aged 3 to 11 is shown below and can be modified for older pupils (see page 68).

12. The data from the pupil questionnaires and the school summary record is used to determine the frequency, severity, nature and place of bullying activities in and around each school.

Questionnaire Material (Attitudes Towards Victims): When the time comes to begin the intervention programme it will be necessary to examine the attitudes held by children about victims. The main reason for this is that the issues of forming good social relationships, social cooperation and empathy are important aspects of the personal/social curriculum for all pupils. Bullying is the negation of these three vital social skills and should be made into a curriculum issue, particularly in those communities where there is a high frequency of bullying. It is of the utmost value to teachers to learn just how bullies and victims are perceived by the pupils. This will help to focus this personal and social curriculum content more sharply.

As described in Chapter 1 there has been considerable interest in the attitudes of children to bullying, or more specifically to the victims of bullying. Responses to the questionnaires mentioned in that chapter clearly give teachers vital information about the ways in which the pupils of their school perceive victims. These attitudes may need modification through counselling or curriculum input. The questionnaire below is given with the permission of the author, Dr. Ken Rigby. It consists of the twenty items used by Rigby and Slee (1991) and tap attitudes towards victims. To

CONFIDENTIAL

SCHOOL SURVEY ON BULLYING

Teacher checklist/survey

For the purposes of completing the checklist bullying is defined as :

> The behaviour arising from the deliberate intent to cause physical or psychological distress to others or to extort something from them.

What is the age range of your class?

....

How many pupils do you have in your class?
Boys .... Girls .... Total ....

In your opinion how many pupils in your class :

1. Are disliked by the majority of others?
   ....

2. Are known bullies? ....

3. Are known victims? ....

4. Are potential bullies? ....

5. Are potential victims? ....

6. Are difficult to control? ....

7. Have frequent tantrums? ....

8. Frequently fight/hit/kick/bite other children?
   ....

9. Are deliberately destructive to other people's/pupil/s property? ....

10. Frequently taunt/tease or are spiteful to other children? ....

11. Call people unpleasant names?..

At what age do you think bullying Starts? ....

Stops? ....

Is most widespread? ....

Have you dealt with a bullying problem?

Yes ❑

No ❑

Do you feel you were successful? Yes ❑

No ❑

Do you feel you need any specific training to help you to deal with bullying problems?

Additional comments.

Thank You

SCHOOL SUMMARY SHEET
Name of School

Summary of Teachers' Checklist

Boys Girls Total

1. Number of children surveyed age 3-5 years?

2. Number of children surveyed age 3-7 years?

3. Number of children surveyed age 7-9 years?

4. Number of children surveyed age 9-11 years?

Questions	2	3	4	5	6	7	8	
BOYS								
3-5 years								
5-7 years								
7-9 years								
9-11 years								
GIRLS								
3-5 years								
5-7 years								
7-9 years								
9-11 years								

use their own description; 'half the items were positively keyed (eg 'weak kids need help'), and half were negatively keyed (eg 'nobody likes a wimp')'. Three response categories were provided for each item: agree, unsure, and disagree. Total scores in the direction of support for victims may, therefore, range from 20 to 60, the lower the score, the worse a pupil's attitude to victims is likely to be.

Children are told *not* to give their names.

Attitudes to Bullying Questionnaire

Please tick here if you are a GIRL ❑
Please tick here if you are a BOY ❑

In this part you will be asked some questions which you should answer yourself, without discussion with anyone. *Please try not to miss out any questions.*

You will not be asked to give your name, so no-one will know who has answered this questionnaire. Just say what you really think.

Now read each one of these sentences carefully and show how strongly you agree or disagree with it. Do this by circling *one* of the answers written underneath it:

1   Kids who get picked on a lot usually deserve it

    Your answer: Agree   Unsure   Disagree

2   Weak kids need help

    Your answer: Agree   Unsure   Disagree

3   It is funny to see kids get upset when they are teased

    Your answer: Agree   Unsure   Disagree

4   When someone is being pushed around, it is best to take no notice

    Your answer: Agree   Unsure   Disagree

5   Kids who hurt others weaker than themselves should be told off

    Your answer: Agree   Unsure   Disagree

6   Nobody likes a wimp

Your answer: Agree   Unsure   Disagree

7   You should not pick on someone who is weaker than you

Your answer: Agree   Unsure   Disagree

8   It makes me angry when a kid is picked on for no reason

Your answer: Agree   Unsure   Disagree

9   I wouldn't be friends with kids who let themselves be pushed around

Your answer: Agree   Unsure   Disagree

10 You shouldn't make fun of people who don't fight back

Your answer: Agree   Unsure   Disagree

11 Kids who are weak are just asking for trouble

Your answer: Agree   Unsure   Disagree

12 It's a good thing to help children who can't defend themselves

Your answer: Agree   Unsure   Disagree

13 I like it when someone stands up for kids who are being bullied

Your answer: Agree   Unsure   Disagree

14 I don't think much of big kids who throw their weight around

Your answer: Agree   Unsure   Disagree

15 I can't stand kids who keep running to the teacher when somebody teases them

Your answer: Agree   Unsure   Disagree

16 Kids should not complain about being bullied

Your answer: Agree   Unsure   Disagree

17 A bully is really a coward

> **Your answer:**   Agree   Unsure   Disagree

18 Soft kids make me sick

> **Your answer:**   Agree   Unsure   Disagree

19 It's OK to call some kids nasty names

> **Your answer:**   Agree   Unsure   Disagree

20 Some of my friends get bullied

> **Your answer:**   Agree   Unsure   Disagree

The results obtained using this questionnaire by this writer are discussed in Chapter 1 and may be used as a benchmark for other surveys.

Interviews: Staff, pupil and parent interviews offer a rich vein of qualitative data and will provide details on the following:

- bullying 'hotspots' in and around the schools,

- information on grudge bearing families or pupil groups that are expressed as bullying,

- greater insights into why bullying occurs in certain areas or in association with certain events,

- invaluable suggestions about improving the physical problems of the school that contribute to bullying,

- vital information on gender, disability and racial bullying,

- ideas about what should be done,

- pointers to what has been done that worked and why,

- the opportunity to counsel victims (including adults) and help to restore lost confidence and self-esteem,

- the exposure of hitherto unknown bullies, and

- vital information (with permission) for case studies to be used in training and with the local media.

Staff Interviews: These should come before pupil interviews and, in the case of teachers, should be structured around the responses made to the teacher questionnaire. The object of this exercise is to help teachers expand on information they are given and to encourage them to present their own ideas for change in an open discussion. As a consequence the interview has both a structured and unstructured component.

Do not ignore non-teaching staff, particularly lunch-times supervisors, who will have equally valid view points arising from their experiences during one of the worst bullying times in the school day. Non-teaching assistants, secretaries and caretakers will also have their own unique perspective on bullying and can make very useful suggestions for improvement.

Parent Interviews: These should take place with three categories of parents;

- parents of bullies

- parents of victim

- neutral parents

Care must be taken from the outset that parents are encouraged to feel relaxed and part of a genuine attempt to help them and their children. The parents of bullies should not feel intimidated or challenged and a few minutes explanation how they can assist does much to help them feel valued despite their offsprings' errant ways.

The parents of bullies have much to tell you about the causes of bullying. Explanations that they give provide important material for anti-bullying literature for all parents. Some of the more common points they raise include:

- 'We have always taught him to hit first',

- 'We didn't want her to be walked on so we encouraged her to try and win all the time',

- 'His elder brother always pushed him around so we told him to get angry first with people',

- 'She's seen my wife and me fighting with each other day after day',

- 'My husband's been a right bully all his life',

- 'The local lads are always bullying him — he just follows their example with smaller kids',

- 'Only the tough survive these days'.

The parents of victims provide equally helpful material, particularly in respect of the 'symptoms' of bullying. Since nearly half of all victims do not tell people spontaneously (Randall and Donohue, 1993) it is helpful to use direct quotes in parents' literature. Parents typically report the following warning signs:

- not wanting to go to school

- avoiding particular lessons or days

- taking long or different routes to and from school

- being late for school, hanging back or returning late from school

- having 'mystery illnesses' — non-specific pains, tummy upsets, headaches

- having unexplained cuts and bruises

- torn and damaged clothing or belongings

- 'mislaid' books, equipment and belongings

- asking for extra money or sweets without giving clear reasons

- personality changes — irritable, withdrawn, tired, poor sleeping, weeping, crying outbursts, loss of appetite, forgetfulness, distractibility

- temper outbursts, abusive language, impulsive hitting out

- lack of confidence, making excuses for not going out to play or meeting other children

- nightmares

- bed-wetting

Neutral parents, those that are neither the parents of bullies nor victims, can provide excellent material from a dispassionate viewpoint. Their observations are generally balanced and, whilst decrying bullying, frequently provide insights why certain victims attract bullying and need to change the ways in which they present themselves. Material based upon them is less likely to be perceived as a set of professional opinions about '...how people should live' being forced on parents.

Pupil Interviews: These interviews must be conducted in a relaxed and warm fashion. Bullies should not be interrogated and victims should be encouraged to lose any feelings of shame that they might hold. It is generally better that both are not interviewed by their own teacher or parent but by a warm, friendly adult who is not known to them or even an older pupil who is empathetic. The relationship between interviewee and interviewer is crucial as pupils should feel that they do not have to lie in order to either avoid punishment or please the interviewer. Other tips for a successful interview include:

- Use 'neutral territory', a room that is not threatening and is free of interruptions and negative associations,

- Give a good explanation of the purpose and praise the pupil for being helpful,

- Do not be afraid to 'identify' with the pupil by recounting your own experiences of being a bully or a victim,

- Be prepared for signs of emotion; anxiety, anger or fear. Allow the pupil to express these emotions,

- Be prepared to counsel any pupil who needs it or to make clear arrangements for providing such help,

- Do not press for details the pupils are unwilling to give. Particularly do not probe for details of family relationships that you may feel are influential to certain bullying activities,

- Deal with any disclosure of abuse by immediately initiating the agreed procedures for your area,

- Finish the session as happily as possible and always agree to see the pupils again if they ask.

Finally it is worth noting that some researchers in the area of bullying invite peer nominations. Sharp and Smith (1994), for example, suggest that pupils are each asked to write down the names of three boys and three girls in their classes, 'who:

- have a lot of friends;

- are happy in school;

- get picked on a lot by other pupils;

- pick on other pupils a lot' (p.17).

These authors advocate that these pupils who were regularly nominated for either or both of the last two categories should be noted because they are likely to be involved with bullying activities, either as bullies or victims, sometimes both. Such children could be interviewed gently to determine what characteristics they have that attracts such a shared opinion within their class.

Completing the Bully Audit in The Schools

The final report should bind together the information in an easily accessible fashion for each school in the targeted community and also provide an embracing 'All Schools' report. Vital features of the reports include:

- frequency of bullying

- severity of bullying

- hotspots, in and out of schools

- attitudes to victims

- a profile of bullies

- a profile of victims

- community factors causing bullying in an out of schools

- case study profiles of bullies and victims

- suggestions for change from

  pupils

  parents

  staff, and

- recommendations for action for each school.

CHAPTER 5

The bully audit in the community

Introduction

Many adults believe that bullying is a problem for children and young people only and, as we have seen, largely blame schools for the problem. The point has already been made of whatever goes on in schools is only the visible tip of the iceberg; hidden below the social waterline is the aggression running through the community that enters the schools that serve it. It takes many forms; unpleasant gossip around the tea table when children hear their parents condemn other adults; racial slurs and petty jealousies that become exaggerated into hate filled invective; envy of those who are better off materially and often a holier-than-thou attitude that becomes aggressive. As adults we are all aware of the undercurrents of enmity between adults that can surface in the behaviour of their children. It is from such feelings that bullying can arise; as one bully said 'I reckoned it was OK to keep pushing and thumping him around, after all my Mam said the whole family are just a bunch of gypsies". The spitefulness of neighbours can set the scene for severe bullying, particularly when people live on top of each other in densely packed urban areas. Take this example:

> Jane is terrified of her neighbours. 'I've only to put my foot outside the door and they start shouting abuse at me. The language is foul and my little boy has started to repeat it at school. They've put horrible things through my letter box and emptied dustbins in my front garden.

Often they draw their cars up outside and play the car radios as loud as they can — they know I've got a baby and it wakes her up. They pick on me because I'm on my own and haven't got a man here to stop them. What's worse is that their kids have now started bullying my son at school. They don't know why — they've just started copying their parents'.

Such events pollute the daily transactions of the community and initiate the tragedies enacted within schools. It is the nature, frequency and impact of these events that must be uncovered by the community bullying audit. This is best carried out as part of a profiling process designed to illuminate the particular needs of the community in respect of bullying.

Needs Assessment

The needs of a community with regard to the events and circumstances of bullying are one of many non-physical needs a community can have. This section continues with a broad examination of the concept of needs in the context of communities.

Non-physical needs such as social and educational needs are notoriously difficult to pin down and constitute a topic about which people from every walk of life and many different professions all have differing opinions. For example, in relation to community services, members of the community (or clients) will tell researchers what their problems are and what sort of help they want, service providers may share these views but frequently differ on what is best to be delivered for the clients and they also have their own needs. Finance managers argue from the view point of invested interest and are unwilling to define needs in such a manner that threatens to tie up a lot of capital. In addition, it has been argued that the caring professionals often tell clients what their problems are and what they need without seeking an opinion from the clients themselves (Bradshaw, 1992).

It is not surprising therefore that social and educational needs, like those associated with health, are now firmly a linked political problem at both national and local level and the way they are defined has repercussions both for those who need help and those who fund and provide it. It is as a consequence of this that arguments rage between politicians, providers and clients about the concept of 'unmet need' which are precisely those types of need that many victims of bullying express across the country; 'No-one listens to what we say about this estate. You take your life in your hands when you go out this front door'.

It is clear that need cannot be determined by opinions or epidemiology alone. In its guidance to managers the DoH (1991) defines need in terms of 'the requirements of individuals of quality of life'. This definition looks at needs in terms of outcomes, although it also begs the question as to what is an acceptable level? In an attempt to try and answer the problems it is necessary to examine some different concepts of need.

It would be overly simplistic to try and apply a simple structured hierarchy of needs (of the type proposed by the psychological Maslow) to this situation1. Although there are clear requirements concerning physio-logical, safety and security needs, the higher level needs such as social activity, esteem and self-realisation defy agreed definition. One finds reference to these higher level needs in the mission statements of pro-viders and in many local authority policy statements but, in actuality, providers are only required by law to satisfy the lowest levels of Maslow's hierarchy.

Bradshaw (1992) has subdivided social need into four elements as follows:

1. NORMATIVE — a standard laid down by professional expertise.

2. FELT — a subjective 'want' of a service but unstated.

3. EXPRESSED — a stated 'want:, the felt need is turned into action.

4. COMPARATIVE — the difference between those who qualify and receive services and those who qualify but do not get them.

Although this subdivision of need does not help to prioritise in the same way that a hierarchical structure does, it does help us to understand how the social/educational need is being defined. There is an argument that a 'real' need would only exist if all four elements were present, but in certain circumstances a 'real' need may not always be felt or expressed by the subject (e.g., an elderly person with advanced senile dementia). There is also room for a dynamic interplay between professional 'normative' definitions of need and subjective 'felt' and 'expressed' definitions of need given by clients.

Putting together these hierarchical and conceptual classifications leads to a more balanced approach for the purposes of assessment and survey. A purely epidemiological analysis would yield only a comparative element. Measurement to a professionally set standard will give a purely normative view and reacting simply to clients' views would give only a subjective 'want' list. None of these would be satisfactory within a community empowerment project of this type. To obtain a more comprehensive view we need to take each into account and then, when planning a response to those needs (or recommending a response to those needs), prioritise them according to a hierarchical model which is defensible.

Recently a project which uniquely combined the four Bradshaw categories has been carried out in Northern Ireland. The Needs Assessment Research Project (NARP) used a three-point dynamic between clients, data and key informants which is simply represented as follows:

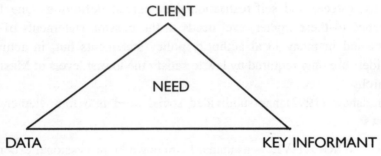

FIG 1 — The NARP Model of Need (Armstrong & Little, 1993)

Thus bullying related needs would be examined from three perspectives:

1. Data-Epidemiological patterns

2. Key informant — reports of incidence and severity by those working in the field (i.e., health visitors, social workers, youth leaders, etc.

3. Client — self-reported definitions of the problems experienced by a variety of people spanning the community and of a wide age range.

Community Profiling

If the model of description of social need given above is accepted then the community bullying audit must be designed to gather data in a manner which may be systematically utilised by that model. We already know that inconsistency is very probable given the gross individual variations that exist in relation to, for example, the understanding of what bullying is, funding arrangements, staffing of professional services and prevalence of voluntary section support, to name but a few. This variation must be controlled for and, in moving from model to practice, we must ensure a design that is simple for non-professional people without significant training to use, is robust and defensible against those who wish to challenge it and is easily replicable. *Community Profiling* is one method or set of methods that will meet the requirements of this needs model and the requirements of practicality. A brief introduction to the history and process of this is now given.

What is Community Profiling?

In recent years many of the traditional notions of service delivery by statutory agencies, particularly local authorities, have been challenged. The challenge has come mainly from central government which is constantly looking for greater value for money from the public purse. But there has also been a growth in consumerism, where local people have begun to be more assertive in saying what services they want, how they want them provided and who they want to be involved in provision. Underlining both of these developments is a growing commitment to improving the quality of service provision and to achieving greater equality in the distribution of services. Bullying is often seen to arise from inequalities of opportunity and the allocation of resources.

As a consequence a wide range of new partnerships are developing to plan and provide local services. These involve health, education, social services, and urban regeneration agencies. Each of these new partnerships attaches a great significance to the accurate identification of needs (however they choose to define need). The concept of partnership, however, is also beginning to characterise the process of identifying and articulating the expression of need. There is a growing recognition that it is better to involve potential consumers in this process then to treat them as passive individuals that do little more than tick little boxes on a questionnaire. As may be seen above the NARP model makes extensive use of an active partnership.

Community Profiling is a term used to describe an approach to identifying needs which emphasises the importance of the partnership. The partnership must involve those with allegedly unmet need and who would consume services if they were available and also those who plan those services, monitor their effectiveness and regulate their delivery.

Unfortunately community profiling is not without its own confusions and ambiguities and the first step towards success is to ensure a consistent understanding across the partnerships. For this reason, community profiling is best considered in terms of local teams running particular projects. The survey of needs in relation to bullying should therefore, for each area, cover three main elements:

- a social, environmental and economic description

- of the targeted community

- which is used to inform local decision making.

It is clear from this that the conduct of the bullying audit also gives rise to the network of people who can carry through the project.

Community profiling may be seen as having ten steps (Burton, 1993), as follows:

Step 1	Assembling a group
Step 2	Initial prioritising
Step 3	Initial planning and time scale setting
Step 4	Mobilising resources
Step 5	Gathering data
Step 6	Analysing data and identifying needs
Step 7	Presenting results
Step 8	Taking the results forward
Step 9	Working with others to create resources
Step 10	Monitoring and evaluation

The first six of these constitute the bullying audit work in the community; the last four utilise the network established to design and implement the programme.

Step One: Putting the Audit Group Together

Assembling a group of co-workers as an Implementation Group for the project has already been described in an earlier chapter 3. This first step is the most important for the community profile process; after all if a group of people willing to work together cannot be assembled then the project is unable to go ahead. It may be necessary however for the Implementation Group discussed previously to be split into different groups for different reasons. One could be given responsibility for carrying out community profile for bullying. On the assumption that that is the case, it is then necessary to determine what sort of constitution this Audit Group should have.

The Audit Group: If very small it is most important that this group has at least one local resident on it and preferably someone who has one or more children attending the local schools. If the Audit Group is to consist of more than three people then it should have at least two residents to form a partnership with two or more professionals from the area. Indeed it is the case that all groups formed from within the Implementation Group should have a clear sense of partnership involving both residents and professionals. A 'mission statement' of one such group reflects this. 'To create a healthier, safer community for people to live and work in securely and happily'.

Since the audit work will demand meeting and conversing with many different people in a variety of settings throughout the community it is obviously necessary that people chosen for the Audit Group should have an enthusiasm for listening to people as well as the social skills necessary to extract information in a sufficiently harmonious way that leaves both the interviewee and the interviewer satisfied and at ease. If the community is ridden with different 'territorial groups' or sects that rarely communicate well with each other then it is necessary for the Audit Group to consist of people who have credibility with these different subsets of the community. It is vitally important that the community audit is carried out across the community and does not favour any particular part of it. In general terms the best people to have for the audit purpose are those who expressed interest in the community profiling process, want to know more about the area and hope that the profile obtained will improve aspects of life for everyone.

The professionals chosen for the Audit Group can be any who:

- work extensively in the community and know it well,

- have credibility with the residents,

- are well known to and respected by the professional institutions such as schools and health centres, and

- have the opportunity to contribute consistently during the time that the audit is underway.

Some professionals have one or more of these characteristics but lack the latter for consistent input. They may have a useful contribution to make to other groups from within the Implementation Group but may not be able to find the time to carry out the exhaustive interviews and survey work for the audit. An earlier section has already listed some potentially useful professionals for the Implementation Group and the same list is applicable here for the Audit Group. They might include a housing officer, social workers, health visitors or general practitioners, librarians, teachers and youth workers. Police liaison officers also have an important contribution to make and their presence in the Audit Group may be a demonstration to local people that there is a desire to do something about the kind of aggression that makes a community unpleasant to live in. Other members of the Audit Group could usefully be drawn from the voluntary sector groups operating within the community. These could include the organisers of parent and toddler clubs, playgroup leaders, victim support workers and church groups. Each one of these may have a unique contribution to make and a very detailed understanding of some of the unmet needs that the community may have in relation to the fear, anxiety and degradation caused by neighbourhood bullying.

It may be helpful to have an elected representative present on the Audit Group. Such people often have access to resources through various committees they sit on and to include them in the Audit Group may bring home to them and therefore, to the committees they represent, the size and scale of the problem in the targeted community.

Forming the Group

Once the group is established it is very necessary to keep it established, at least until the bully audit work is complete. The Audit Group, as a number of people representing a wide spectrum of the community's interests, will have very different experiences of meetings and very different understandings of how they should proceed. It is probable that certain factors arise that will contribute to feelings of unease and eventually disillusionment of the group. In addition there may be many practical problems that will hinder regular meetings and regular work in the community. These factors should be identified and resolved as quickly as possible. Here are a few common causes for such groups to fragment without achieving their purpose:

- the venue for the meetings is not accessible to some of the people — if necessary combat this problem by having different venues reflecting different needs.

- some people have to look after children — can a creche be organised?

- meetings are held at the wrong time — it isn't generally possible to suit all group members all of the time but varying the time of the meeting may mean that the majority of the people on the group can be present for most meetings.

- people find it difficult to come to the venues because of transport problems — is it possible to identify a small budget for taxis?

- some members of the group are not made to feel welcome by others — is there a problem of one-upmanship? Perhaps some of the professional people feel the local resident representatives are inferior, is it therefore possible to have a private word about this? Do the elected representatives try to dominate the professionals — can they be encouraged to share their skills and local knowledge?

- the meetings are all talk and/or are confusing — ensure that there are ground rules for the meetings that prevent this from happening.

- the meetings don't lead to action — ensure that there are deadlines and action plans from each meeting so that people have a clear understanding of what must be achieved by when.

It is clear from this that resources should be identified to make the meetings as 'comfortable' as possible. In addition ground rules need to be established from the outset which will prevent the meetings from turning into boring and unproductive events. The Audit Group must meet for its purpose and not just simply for sake of the meeting. Be wary of introducing too much formality or pomposity into the Audit Group meetings, it is not a mortal sin if a meeting is not properly minuted or properly chaired as long as the objectives are met. A few simple rules will, however, help to ease the passage of each meeting:

- only one person to talk as once.

- everyone has same rights of veto whether they be elected representatives, professionals or local residents.

- the timetable for meetings will always be upheld. Decision can only be taken if the group is quorate.

The first meeting of the group should decide upon these rules and other aspects of group organisation. It is important to decide:

- if the group will allow other people to join the meetings for a specific purpose, such as the provision of specialist information.

- to confirm the membership of the group and, if necessary, to add to it.

- if the group is going to have a person leading it, perhaps a chairperson, who should that person be?

- all the group members should have agendas and minutes (or notes) of each session. Who will produce these?

- how often will the group meet and under what circumstances can special meetings be called?

- apart from members of the group who else will see the minutes of each meeting (presumably the Audit Group will be reporting back to the full Implementation Group).

- what will be done about conflicts and resolutions (it is normal to put such matters to a vote and accept a majority)?

- does any member of the group need any personal circumstance to be taken into account (for example, one member may wish to leave the meeting when difficulties associated with a school their child attends are raised).

Step Two: Prioritising the Work of the Audit Group

Once the first meeting of the group has resolved its rules and organisational processes as described in Step One it will next need to consider its brief in detail. It is probable that the Implementation Group will have set the brief for the Audit Group in a general way but it is necessary for the Audit Group to specify this detail and produce a working plan for meeting the specific requirements.

The methods of achieving specific objectives should be listed according to Aims, Objectives and Methods. For example:

AIMS	Identify bullying activities in the shopping centre.
OBJECTIVES	1. Determine daily rate of observed bullying. 2. Interview at least 10 victims 3. Find out if the bullies are usually the same ones.
METHODS	Interview at least 75% of shop managers and shop assistants.

When deciding upon Aims, Objectives and Method, it is always desirable to consider the broader ambitions of the Implementation Group for producing this community profile. There are several possible individual motivations for belonging to any sort of group of this type and these often include

- commercial interest
- political interest,
- community interest,
- specific interest in the behaviour of bullying,
- personal interest as a victim or parent of bullying.

It is important that these different motivations should be given full expression and to assist the design of the audit. Any attempt to 'squash' them runs the risk of alienating members of the group and distorting the scope of the audit.

Step Three: Initial Planning and Establishing Timescale

Once there has been a prioritisation of aims, objectives and methods it is possible to move on, either in the same meeting, or at future meetings to draw up strategic plans and set the timescale for completion. To some extent the timescale may be driven by the Implementation Group and since the bully audit in the community is an integral part of the forward planning for the Implementation Group it is likely that the Audit Group will have to produce its findings in a relatively short space of time. This should not however be allowed to detract from a process whereby local residents are given opportunity to voice their opinions having been given due warning that their opinions will be asked for. For example, the opinions of elders living in the community are vital because it is often the case that they are subjected to bullying and generally harassing activities from a minority of other people. It is necessary to allow at least a week for elders to be notified that their opinion will be sought and at what time and by whom. This allows them the opportunity to refuse the interview or to prepare for it by marshalling their opinions and arguments.

It is impossible to plan the time of the Audit Group effectively without having a clear idea of what is to be achieved and how it is to be achieved. It may be necessary to make a choice between:

- trying to achieve as many aims of the group by a particular deadline and ignoring aims of lesser importance when time runs out;
- working on all the aims and ensuring that sufficient time is given to each.

If the latter approach is taken the Implementation Group as a whole must be prepared to either suspend its activities or proceed in other directions whilst the Audit Group completes its work. Whatever approach is taken it is important that each meeting of the Audit Group produces a timescale and considers whether or not it is working within that timescale.

Step Four: Identifying Necessary Resources

Once the group is assembled, its priorities set and linked to an initial timescale, the Audit Group must consider what resources are required in order to meet its aims. One of the best ways is to ask each group member to identify required resources before a particular meeting. It is then only necessary to create a summary list of all these individual lists. There should be no debate about the value of particular items listed at this stage; the lists are merely collated and used as the basis for further discussion. It is helpful if each individual member uses a common format as follows:

Resources	Date	Need
Meeting Rooms		
Transport		
Equipment		
Photocopier		
Tape Recorders		
Computer & Printer		
etc.		
Budgets		
Time		
Expertise		
Local knowledge		
Local contacts		
Political influence		

The list given above is fairly typical but it is by no means exhaustive. For example, because of the problems of travelling of individual members it might be necessary to identify more than one meeting place in order that those members can be accommodated more easily on some meetings than others. It may also be decided by that the interview sessions with potential victims in the community might be best video recorded in which case it would be necessary to obtain a camcorder and VCR. It is important, also, to list seemingly prosaic resources such as having sufficient pens, paper, audio cassette tapes and so forth in order that the audit process can go smoothly.

Once the summary list of resources has been drawn up members of the group must understand that it is not cast in tablets of stone, it can be revised whenever necessary.

At the same meeting, or the next one, it is necessary to discuss how to fill gaps in the resources. It may be that some gaps have to be accepted and the group must work without the benefits of the resource. On the other hand it may be possible to fill some gaps by borrowing equipment. Thus, for example, having sufficient meeting places to suit every group member's needs may be resolved by asking headteachers of the local schools to provide a place for the meetings on a rotation basis. The same head-teachers may also have access to video equipment.

Step Five: Gathering the Data

The Audit Group must have a shared understanding of what data is to be collected and how it is to be analysed. Some members of the group may mistakenly believe that data is all about statistics; numbers which are manipulated to provide some kind of summary information. Numerical data is sometimes referred to as hard data, such as the number of instances of bullying taking place outside a particular group of shops each day over a three week period. This sort of data is clearly highly descriptive and extremely useful. Soft data, however, can be equally as useful depending on the purposes for which it is being collected. Soft data includes peoples' impressions, opinions and perceptions as well as their feelings, experiences and beliefs. This sort of data can be useful in putting a 'human' face to the hard data, although it can never replace it. In the next chapter concerning the use of the media, this data will be shown to be particularly important.

The group must also realise that there is no point in gathering data unless something is done with it. Data is generally used in community profiling to support arguments, to describe events and circumstances and to back up ideas. In making recommendations to the Implementation Group the Audit Group will be using data to demonstrate that these recommendations are worth considering.

It would be helpful to prioritise it to show which recommendations;

• are vital for implementation,

• which are desirable for implementation, and

• which should be implemented if resources require them to do so.

Existing Data: The frequency of bullying in the community at all ages is strongly related to socioeconomic characteristics of the community. In general terms there is more bullying and harassment to be found in communities where there is deprivation, disadvantage and high levels of unemployment. Frustrated needy people are more likely to show aggression than happy, content and materially advantaged people. It is therefore necessary for the Audit Group to be able to 'describe' the community by using existing data. The kind of data that is useful for this description includes:

- the rate of unemployment

- statistics on crimes of violence

- divorce rate

- statistics on addictions

- the numbers of children on free school meals (a popular index of material disadvantage)

- the numbers of single parent families, and

- the age distribution of the community.

Many of these statistics will be available locally as small area statistics produced from the 1991 census. They may be obtained by contacting a researcher within the local authority or a good community librarian.

Collecting Hard Data: It is generally helpful to have only one or two questionnaires with which to go out into the community to determine peoples feelings about bullying and to gain an estimation of its frequency. A suitable survey questionnaire is shown below:

Collecting Soft Data: Video or audio tape could be used extremely effectively to record people's experiences of bullying. A video can be made of bullying activities occurring in community hotpots, for example, outside newsagents or fish and chip shops where a lot of bullying of young people by other young people occurs. Video tapes of young people coming out of school may also be useful in demonstrating how that particular time of the day may be associated with an increase with bullying incidents. Likewise, video tapes made of playground or park activities might also be helpful in revealing other aspects of bullying in the community.

Recording interviews with victims can have a very hard hitting impact on resource controllers such as politicians and the soft data gathered by the Audit Group should always include either video or carefully noted interviews with victims of all ages.

POPULATION SURVEY QUESTIONNAIRE

Please indicate with a tick if you are

Male ❑ or Female ❑

Please indicate your age by ticking one of the following:

Less than 18   18-25   25-35   35-45   45-55   55-65
              65-75   Older than 75

How long have you lived in this area, please tick one of the following:

Less than 5 years 5-10 years   10-15 years 15-20 years

Longer that 20 years

Do you see much evidence of child bullying?   YES or NO

If YES, can you describe it?

Do you see much evidence of adult bullying (eg. harassing neighbours, verbal abuse, physical abuse, damage to property, etc)? YES or NO

If YES, can you describe it?

What do you think causes bullying in the area?

What do you think should be done about it?

If you are a parent or grandparent, do you worry about the possibility of your children or grandchildren being bullied?   YES NO

Do you feel that some children become bullies because of the behaviour they witness at home?   YES NO

If you saw a child being bullied in the street by a gang, what could you realistically do about it?

How much of the following are you aware of:

Drug use/drug dealing	OFTEN	SOMETIMES	NEVER
Aggressive neighbours	OFTEN	SOMETIMES	NEVER
Gangs of youths	OFTEN	SOMETIMES	NEVER
Vandalism/graffiti	OFTEN	SOMETIMES	NEVER
Nuisance from drunks	OFTEN	SOMETIMES	NEVER
Uncontrolled children	OFTEN	SOMETIMES	NEVER
Video/TV violence acted out in children's behaviour	OFTEN	SOMETIMES	NEVER

Educational or school related problems (Please give details)

	OFTEN	SOMETIMES	NEVER

Have you been attacked?   YES   NO

Insulted?   YES   NO

Had property damaged?   YES   NO

We would really like to have your ideas about how to stop bullying in the community. What could we do to help? Please put your ideas on a separate piece of paper. Don't forget to put you name and address on it, a prize could be yours.

IF YOU OWN OR WORK IN A SHOP IN THE AREA PLEASE COULD YOU ALSO COMPLETE THIS SECTION

Are you aware of bullying inside/outside your premises?   YES NO

Is it the same bullies most times or different ones?   YES NO

What impact does this have on business?

What could shop workers do to help to help prevent bullying?

What could be done to help shop workers?

It is necessary for the group to think carefully about why it needs or wants some information and the way that information should be presented. The the Audit Group will need to work out how often bullying occurs, for example, outside the local 'hotspots' like an off-license and to report that this occurs on average X times a week; it also makes sense for this figure X to be brought to life by a video recording of bullying incidents occurring outside that off-license.

It is a good idea to allow data collection to mushroom. As one type of information is collected so it may indicate that other types are possibly valuable. In general it is wise to work from the broad survey questionnaire approach shown above through to increasingly detailed personal experiences and opinions.

Surveys

Surveys can be simple or complicated, some are inexpensive whereas others may demand a lot of resources. Some can be carried out within days whilst others may be more protracted. It is important that the Audit Group designs its survey carefully according to the resources available, its timescale and, of course, the characteristics of the people who will be contributing data.

The headings and guidelines that follow provide general information about the design and implementation of surveys, they will not relate to all communities everywhere so some tailoring will be necessary.

Surveys obviously involve asking people a range of questions. Therefore it is necessary to know:

- whom to ask questions of;

- what questions to ask them;

- how the questions will be asked.

Different survey questionnaires may be needed depending on the answers to these questions. It is often possible to devise a general purpose questionnaire (as is the case above) which can be used out on the street simply by stopping people at random or according to preselected criteria of age, race, gender and other characteristics and also in GP surgeries, shops, offices, schools and other institutions in the community. Where an all purpose questionnaire has been devised it may also be possible to use it in telephone surveys, which represent a relatively quick and efficient means of gaining information. Where disability is an important criterion for selection it is necessary to take steps to include the partially sighted and the hearing impaired through particular venues because such people have difficulty with out-on-the-street survey work.

Where possible it is desirable to gain survey information from households and some interviews involving the survey questionnaire could take place at a time when all the family is present and individual members can contribute their different view points. Household surveys on bullying tap a rich vein of information which spans two and sometimes three generations of people who have experienced life in that community.

When the local media is involved it is perfectly possible to use the all purpose questionnaire in a local newspaper and ask for people to return completed questionnaires to a box number. This does tend to result in a highly selected population responding, usually people who are the victims of bullying, but where they identify themselves they may make themselves available for more intense interviews.

Sampling: This section gives guidance about whom to ask questions.

In part this is dictated by the model of community profiling that is being used. This chapter has put forward the NARP model as effective in completing the bullying audit in the community. It is clear therefore that information must be sampled from a variety of informants that involves not only those people who live in the community but also those who serve it including general practitioners, health visitors and those who provide commercial services such as shopkeepers, garage owners, landlords, pub and club managers. There are also many people in the voluntary sector who may be involved including volunteers in Victim Support, Citizen's Advice Bureau and supportive organisations such as MENCAP, MIND and the Samaritans. Representatives of all these groups can be useful informants.

However, the most important people to sample and gain their opinions are those who live in the community. The Audit Group needs to determine how many people living in the community it must sample to be truly representative and how many it can afford to sample given the resources available. If the resources available enable more than this minimum number of people to be sampled then the additional data will probably be useful; if on the other hand there is insufficient money to sample the minimum number then there is little point in proceeding with the audit.

It is rare that any community project can actually sample the opinion of everyone living in the community. But a sample must be representative of the whole population of people living in the area. Failure to achieve a representative sample will simply result in biased results which are of no value.

Where a sample of the population must be surveyed then it is crucial that the characteristics of the sample are a fair reflection of the characteristics of the population. If, for example, the population as a whole has an average age of 45 then there is little or no sense in selecting a sample with an average age of only 33. Similarly gender distribution and ethnic origin must also be taken into account. The selection characteristics of the sample should pay particular attention to those who have particular difficulties (eg. ethnic communities).

The size of the sample is also important and this largely depends on what is being surveyed. Where the issue is extremely simple or, perhaps, one or two questions only are used then sample size can be smaller than when there are complex issues to be surveyed. Thus a simple poll of voting intentions can be accurate to plus or minus 4% when interviewing only one person in every 24 or 25 thousand. The survey of the type required by the bully Audit Group is, however, much more complex. Given this it is possible to achieve acceptable margins of error (eg. 2-3%) without actually interviewing everyone in the community. There are three preliminaries to determining sample size and type for a particular survey:

- define the population to be sampled, e.g. residents of the Nirvana Street Estate;

- obtain a list of that population, e.g. electoral register or school registers in the case of children; and

- draw the sample using random, stratified or quota methods.

Random or probability sampling: This is the simplest type of sampling method whereby everyone in the sample has an equal chance of being selected. Thus if the total population in the community is 10,000 and a sample size of 100 is required then it is a simple matter to pick every 100th name from the list and sampling frame. This methods assumes people of all types and ages are distributed randomly throughout the list.

Stratified sampling: In this the total sample frame is divided into strata or sections and then individuals are selected at random from each section. Each stratum is generally based upon a particular category such as age, gender or ethnic origin that needs to be covered.

Quota sampling: This is the type of sampling that is most frequently used in on-the-street surveys. In this case the categories are determined in advance and only people who match these criteria are selected. Those who carry out the survey are told how many people in each category to find and it is their responsibility to fill each quota. It is likely that this will be the most suitable sampling for the bully audit.

The questions asked: There are five types of questions that can be asked, each having a different purpose:

- Questions which test the respondent's awareness of a particular problem: 'Do you know somebody who has been bullied recently?'

- Questions which test their feelings on that problem: 'Do you think this area has a bigger bullying problem than elsewhere?'

- Questions to find out how strongly respondent hold certain views: 'Do you think the Youth Club ought to be closed down in order to stop bullying that goes on around it?'

- Questions which establish the respondents' reasons for holding the opinions that they do about bullying: 'Why do you think bullying is potentially harmful to children and young people?'

- Questions to probe particular aspects of bullying: 'What do you think is the biggest single reason for bullying in this area?'.

Asking the questions: Members of the Audit Group may carry out the survey themselves or appoint a team of volunteers to do so. Whoever asks the questions should be clear on some general points.

- Each interviewer should be clear about why the survey is being carried out and how confidential the data is. Much of the information will be sensitive. It could for instance pinpoint particular families as problematic bullies in the area and the respondents will wish their anonymity to be preserved for reasons of personal security. They need to be reassured and to have confidence in the interviewer. Interviewer identification should be available at all times.

- Interviewers must all be clear that they are entirely dependent upon the trust and goodwill of respondents. This means that they do not argue with the respondents even though they may disagree with the views expressed.

- Interviewers should maintain a professionally competent style. This does not rule out friendliness and warmth but it does rule out over-familiarity and identification with respondents.

- Interviewers must record all data honestly and accurately. They should be fully briefed about recording and also be warned not to allow their personal biases and prejudices to be interposed between respondents' responses and the recording.

- Interviewers should have a common format response sheet on which to record responses. This should include a margin where the interviewers can make brief notes if they have problems in interpreting the respondents.

- Interviewers should take part in a peer-appraisal system so that they talk to each other about problems they have encountered and how they have overcome them. This system of support also makes it possible to achieve greater consistency of information gathering.

Drafting the questionnaire: There are a number of design features that the Audit Group should be aware of.

- Start with a clear short explanation of the purpose of the survey and how the information obtained is strictly confidential. This is an example:

  'We would be very grateful for your help. As you will know from the press and radio we want to help children and young people who are badly affected by bullying. It would help us to know how big the problem is and what information people can give us. Please help us help those who are being hurt by bullies. The information you give us is completely confidential — you don't have to give us your full name and no-one but us will know what you've said. Thank you very much for your help'.

- The first question should related directly to these introductory remarks as in this example: 'Do you think there is a lot of bullying in this area?'.   YES   NO

- Questions should flow naturally, that is they should follow a pattern rather than skip from topic to topic. So if for example one question is about bullying on the way to and from school it is sensible that the next question should be about bullying in the school playground or somewhere else on the school premises. It would not be sensible to ask a question about particularly aggressive neighbours!

- Multiple choice questions should have a comprehensive a range of possible answers to enable respondents to feel confident that they can make a choice that accurately reflects their opinions. These choices should not be ambiguous or overlaping.

- Wording is important. People tend to agree rather than disagree when choices are presented starkly — this is a well known acquiescense factor and inevitably distorts the results.

- Specific questions are preferable to general open-ended ones as they reduce the possibility of misinterpretation or individual interpretation.

- Multiple choice and other questions could include the option of 'Don't know' in the range of possible answers. This allows people to adequately display their neutrality.

- The wording of all questions should be checked in a pilot sample.

- This pilot sampling process should also include a check on the accuracy of people who will be scoring, coding or otherwise analysing the data.

- Open questions tap rich sources of opinion but they are always better at the end of the questionnaire than at the front.

- Open questions may well require that the respondents be prompted to give a response. Specific questions tend to get an immediate response.

- Closed questions are easier to score and code.

- Always finish the questionnaire with an open-ended question on the lines of 'Have you any other views on bullying in this area that may be useful to the project?'. The responses to this may well lead into other areas of interest.

- It is important that terminology remains consistent throughout the questionnaire. For example, if the questionnaire refers to 'bullying' is should not for some items be substituted by 'harassing', 'put upon' or 'aggression'. Similarly if the expression 'the local area' is used then it should not be substituted in some items for 'the community'.

- Simple language is essential so:

    Use language as it is written or spoken in the area.

    Use shorter rather than longer words and sentences.

    Avoid double negatives (e.g. 'Do you or do you not agree with the following; teachers should not have to supervise children during lunchtimes'?).

Avoid double-barrelled questions (e.g. 'Do you think play-grounds/shopping centres attract high levels of bullying and why?').

Always put alternatives at the end of a question (e.g. 'Do you avoid dark areas on the estate? Always/often/sometimes/never').

- Avoid jargon and technical concepts.

Avoid using words, phrases or technical expressions which are familiar to professional people but which may well be mis-understood by others.

- Set manageable tasks.

Do not expect people to recall fine detail from an indefinite period in the past. Give them a cut-off point, for example, 'Within the last six months'.

Use 'time marks' wherever possible when asking questions about their past (e.g. since Christmas, last summer).

Do not ask hypothetical questions (e.g. 'If you were the Prime Minister what would you do to stop bullying on the estate?'). Such questions may be given hypothetical answers rather than the real answers that the survey requires.

- The level of information will be extremely variable between respondents. It is often sensible to precede the survey with media coverage that introduces it to local residents and gives them, as far as possible, a shared base of knowledge. Even with this kind of coverage many of the respondents still may not be aware of the project or the need for it and may express surprise that there is interest in bullying.

The Structure of the Interview

Introducing the Survey: Essential points include:

- Interviewers should be confident, firm and obviously committed to the survey. Their introduction should sound convincing and be checked by the survey organisers before they 'hit the streets'. Interviewers who are uncertain, ignorant about the project or confused will provoke a high non-response rate.

- Each interviewer should introduce him or herself properly and carry identification provided by the project.

- Each interviewer should explain the nature and purpose of the survey, reassure respondents about confidentiality and, if necessary, explain why they have been selected for the sample.

Improving participation

Where particular respondents are important to the survey (perhaps because they are victims or bullies) they should be encouraged to take part. This may mean introducing the survey and then coming back at a later time to tackle the questionnaire. When people refuse to participate interviewers should try and find out why, what is deterring them and, if necessary, take steps to make it easier for them to take part. Although interviewers should not harangue people or give the impression that taking part is compulsory they should not be put off by the first refusal but instead develop a short conversation about why the project is important to the community.

Conducting the interview

- The interviewers should ensure that the respondent is comfortable and shielded from rain and cold wherever possible.

- It is permissible to let the respondent see the questionnaire, the answers that are being noted down and be asked to check the information for accuracy.

- Interviewers must stick to the precise wording of each question and the order of the questions.

- Interviewers should not be involved in arguments, discussions or other dialogue with respondents and certainly should not give any impression that they are agreeing or disagreeing with any answers given.

Recording answers

- Interviewers should record complete answers that are relevant. Some respondents will attempt to interpret the question and answer another in the process. Under such circumstances the interviewers should repeat the original question and gently probe for a relevant answer.

- Interviewers must record with clear handwriting, they will not code the responses. The more 'tick boxes' there are in the format the better.

- Pre-coded questions should be ticked or numbered clearly.

- Where the interviewers ask open-ended questions they will have to write in the answer given and as much detail as possible. That means that interviewers must record the actual answer and not their own interpretation. Small hand-held cassette recorders can be useful but tend to be off-putting.

Finishing the interview

- Interviewers must give respondents the opportunity to ask any final questions about the survey and how the results will be used. It may be that some will want to see the results and the Audit Group will have to have a policy on whether or not the resulting reports will be available for public consumption.

- If an interview has to be terminated before it is fully completed then the respondent should be given a definite time and date for it to recommence.

- Some respondents may want a copy of their interview questionnaire. The Audit Group will have to have a policy about this and it may well be that a photocopy can be sent to the respondent at a later date. Alternatively the questionnaire can be prepared on self-carbonating sheets so a tear-off copy can be given immediately.

- All interviewers should check each interview questionnaire immediately after the termination of the interview and return the completed questionnaire to the Audit Group as soon as possible.

Piloting the Survey

As as been mentioned it is a good idea to run a small pilot survey before the proper survey commences. This gives opportunities to detect and resolve problems before they obscure or distort the results. Such a pilot will also allow the questionnaire to be tested when difficulties in its structure and form are revealed. The results from the pilot study can be used provided that the sample for the pilot matches the proper survey sample and the data obtained is compatible with that obtained later from the main survey.

Respondents and interviewers taking part in the pilot should be asked the following questions:

- Did you or the respondent feel uncomfortable about asking/being asked any of the questions, if so

— which?

— why?

— how would you suggest changing them?

- Was it necessary to repeat any questions?

- Where any questions regularly misinterpreted by the respondents?

- Where any questions particularly difficult to ask?

Why?

How could they be changed?

- Did any of the parts of the questionnaire or sets of questions seem to be a waste of time? Why?

- Where there any questions or set of questions that the respondents would have liked to have said more about?

The pilot survey also gives an opportunity to train interviewers effectively.

One of the best ways of training people about carrying out this kind of survey is to supervise them doing fieldwork using people with good experience of similar work as supervisors.

The briefing for interviewers needs to be simple but complete. It is generally necessary to include the following:

- The quota sample to be selected;

- A brief explanation of the project and why the survey is important.

- What particular terms and phrases mean within the questionnaire;

- How to make use of any coding systems that some questions require;

- How to use a skip system within the questionnaire if it exists (eg. 'If the answer to this question is 'yes' please go straight to question 10').

This kind of training should be done in small groups with opportunity for one-to-one supervision as necessary. Interviewers at this stage of their training should be given opportunity for questions and discussion in order that any concerns they may have are resolved early on rather than when they are 'out on the street'. Interviewers must also be made aware of the particular importance of:

- confidentiality;

- honesty;

- accuracy.

The workshop sessions should be supported by an interviewer's handbook which contains a complete copy of all the information given plus a list of essential guidelines and also a project manual which contains:

- questionnaires;

- an interview schedule or timetable;

- envelopes and stamps for returning questionnaires to the Audit Group;

- instructions on how to complete the questionnaire;

- spare pens and pencils;

- a map of the local area marked with the particular venues that each interviewer has to cover;

- a large card carrying the name of the person in the Audit Group that the interviewer should make contact with in case of need; and

- an I.D. card and contact numbers for respondents to verify any details they wish.

Finally it is necessary that the police should be aware of the fact that a survey is being carried out. For this reason, if for no other, it is wise to have a police liaison officer on the Implementation Group.

Step Six: Analysing the Data

Data analysis can be complex, costly and time consuming. In community profiling however it is seldom necessary to do more than simple, straight forward cross-tabulations that can be expressed as percentages. The nature of the questionnaire will help to guide this analysis. For example in the questionnaire presented above it would be quite legitimate to make a comment like '33% of women aged between 55 and 65 answered 'Often' to being aware of drug use and drug dealing. This compared with only 5% of women aged between 25 and 35'. Another comment could be 'Over 85% of all men and women surveyed ranging in age from 25 to 75, believed that uncontrolled children were often the cause of aggression in the community'.

Such comments have obvious value, identify needs and are easy to derive. They are also difficult to challenge. Similarly, a comment like '80% of all people over the age of 35 (both men and women) commented that they see much evidence of child bullying', is a clear cut statement that there is a high level of child bullying in the community and therefore a good reason to do something about it.

Qualitative data cannot be handled in such a clear cut way but it can support the percentage cross-tabulation findings. For example, if one of the cross-tabulation comments was '65% of parents worry about the possibility of their children being bullied' then it would be illustrative to add to that comment a piece of qualitative data such as 'For instance, one 35 year old respondent mother told the interviewer that she was so worried about the possibility of her 7 year-old child being bullied that she found it difficult to sleep at night. It was on her mind to such an extent that she was tempted to take her child out of school and educate him at home'.

Whatever form data analysis has taken the aims and objectives of the Audit Group, and therefore of the Implementation Group, must be met. If one of the aims is to create a baseline measure against which future progress be gauged then the Audit Group must present such data clearly in its results.

A final summary of the audit should link directly to the bully audit in schools and the Implementation Group should ensure that a report format enabling this linking is available for the Audit Group to complete. This takes the onus of responsibility away from the Audit Group members, they do not have to divine exactly what it is that the Implementation Group requires.

Note

1   Maslow (1954) proposed a simple heirarchy of human need arguing that needs higher up the hierarchy would not motivate action to meet them if needs lower down were unsatisfied. In descending order these needs were: Self-actualisation (the need to develop our talents and aptitudes), Autonomy (the need to be in control of our lives and events around us), Ego (the need to be valued, liked and respected by others), Social (the need to belong, to be part of a social group), Security (the need to maintain our safety) and Physical (the need for food, water, warmth, reproduction, etc).

CHAPTER 6

Empowerment

The concept and practices of empowerment are central to any community anti-bullying project and it is necessary that core staff, particularly the Implementation Group, should understand them well. This chapter begins with a brief introduction to client empowerment and finishes with a focused examination of its relevance to an anti-bullying programme.

What is Empowerment?

The concept of empowerment has been over-used in descriptions of delivering human services and has lost much of its original meaning. It can simply be defined as 'becoming powerful', but that can mean different things to different people and different social contexts (Adams, 1990). Whatever else it may be, it is always opposed to and works against oppression. Given this it is an ideal flag for an anti-bullying campaign to fly because bullying is, as we have seen, a classic form of oppression of people who are or believe they are, powerless against the bullies.

For now we can accept that empowerment is a process by which individual groups can become more successful in understanding and tackling particular difficulties that beset them. The professionals' role in that is to facilitate the strategies and attitude shifts whereby the individuals or groups can become more powerful. In the context of bullying we can see that if victims become more powerful then they are less likely to be victimised and able to resist the bully.

Even this simple understanding is fraught with difficulties. For example, it seems paradoxical that professionals such are teachers, social workers, psychologists, health visitors and many others become involved with a client group in order to empower them; this implies that the processes are 'owned' by the professionals who bequeath skills to people who lack them. If that is all that empowerment is then it is nothing more than a different form of oppression. Clients simply become beholden to and dependent upon the professional group working with them. In addition, it is also difficult to how to conceptualise the people these professionals are empowering — are they 'clients' in the sense that they have need of professionally delivered personal services, or are they 'trainees' of these professionals in the sense of being trained to do certain things differently or better?

The range of activities that can be part of an empowerment strategy is potentially endless. Almost any professional activity that helps people to help themselves is empowering; thus a doctor who instructs a patient to take medication on a regular basis is empowering that patient to improve his or her health; a marriage guidance counsellor who helps a client to end an abusive relationship is empowering and a residential social worker who supports a group of adults with learning difficulties to function well at their local supermarket is also empowering. The literature of social work and social psychology abounds with excellent examples of empowerment where such considerations are as valued for negatively discriminated communities as for individuals. For example, Ovrebo and colleagues (1995) used health care services for black, pregnant and homeless women to improve their environment and, obviously, that of their unborn children. Roberto, Amburg and Orleans (1995) used community education and social support strategies to empower small 'religious faith' groups in isolated rural communities.

Empowerment is only useful if there is a recognised deficit or power imbalance. This is always the case when bullying is rife wherever it occurs in the community. The deficit lies in the inability of victims to find successful strategies to challenge the power of the bullies over them. Thus, a small group who terrorise a class of pupils has an imbalance of power in their favour in the same way as the charge hand who bullies the women on a food packaging line. This does not mean, however, that there is a simple equation between oppression and empowerment that will correct the balance. First of all it is necessary to consider what characteristics of the oppressed group prevent it from taking control.

The Origins of Powerlessness

In general research studies identify four major deficits or constraints that inhibit the adaptive behaviour of individuals or groups:

- Alienation, being or feeling set apart from the mainstream of society in general or a community in particular;

- Learned Helplessness, becoming excessively dependent so that a capacity for normal functioning is suppressed;

- Locus of Control, the experience or the perception that one's life is controlled by external events or agencies;

- Social-structural disability, perceived or actual deficits that create circumstances where individuals or groups do not have the means to assert themselves despite having the will to do so .

As some or all of these may be present in the targeted community it is necessary that the members of the Implementation Group take account of them when planning empowerment strategies. The following section should make this task easier.

Power and Powerlessness

Birch and Russell (1983) state that the concept of power is fundamental to the social sciences, just as the concept of energy is fundamental to physics. However, the social sciences do not have a single conceptualisation of power. There are many possible conceptualisations and they will differ according to the main focus of investigation. The psychologist will see power in a way which is completely different to that of a political scientist, a sociologist or economist. A social worker whose theoretical background comes from both sociology and psychology will take an eclectic view of power that is very much based on practice. Clarke (1965) made one useful attempt to pull together the various concepts of power in a way that is of particular relevance to bullying. This concept involved relating feelings of powerlessness to lack of self esteem; 'Self-esteem is not determined by forces inherent within the organism but is dependent upon external supports of reinforcements and controlled by the judgments of others who are themselves afflicted with the universal human anxiety of self-doubt'.

External supports and reinforcements for a community invariably include economic and political power factors which function in such a way that they either increase or decrease self-esteem. Such factors that influence individuals to diminish their self-esteem, create vulnerability at both the group and individual levels. This is particularly evident in the context of racism where an ethnic minority group may lose its self-worth because the society in which it functions devalues it, vilifies it and regards it as second class. Individuals within that minority will experience low self-esteem and find it hard to reverse the effects of such oppression.

For similar reasons, a small community living in a street terrorised by a powerful family are relegated by that family to a low status. This is an assault upon the self-esteem of the group worsened by the fact that they cannot stand up to this family and alter the imbalance of power.

In this situation empowerment is best considered as the process whereby a professional group embarks on activities with the community group that aim to reduce powerlessness resulting from the negative valuations of the powerful and oppressive group. These activities are determined by a process whereby the power blocks that contribute to the overall problems are identified and specific strategies are aimed at them. These strategies commonly involve growth and development of those community resources which increase the self-worth of the community. Such resources include schools, civic clubs, volunteer groups, playgroups, parks and other amenities. The better the resources that are developed, the more successful the community will be in finding effective responses to the various problems that beset it.

We must not underestimate the complexity of a relationship between the powerlessness of a group and the negative valuations of that group by another. It may be that the original negative valuations lie in a barely remembered history, as is often the case where there is feuding within the community. One group of people may be seriously undervalued by another group but the reasons for that may have disappeared in the mists of time. All that is left is a general feeling that the group of people who become victims are of lower worth and that there is a permanent 'open season' on them. This fits well with various descriptions given by individual victims who, as some of our examples have shown, realise that the original cause for them becoming victims has long ago been forgotten but that the habit of bullying lingers on. When this kind of phenomenon exists at community level empowerment strategies must address the habit as well as the feelings of low self-esteem.

Further complexity arises that in some communities, groups of individuals have been so exposed to negative valuations that they accept their status as correct. The class structure that appertained until recent times was very much maintained on this belief, the 'Lord of the Manor' was seen as of greater worth than the labourers who farmed his estates.

Where this problem exists, it is often necessary first to convince the powerless group that there is a self-inflicted problem and that they do have rights which are being blocked.

While a community may have significant problems with powerlessness that lead to high risks of bullying, not all individuals within that community will be affected in the same way or even notice the problem. Some negative valuations do not result in powerlessness for individuals within the group. These individuals often have strong family links or are successful in some sphere (e.g. children in deprived areas who do very well in sports or academic pursuits) or have other strength that provides them with a protective cushion against the negative valuations of the larger society. Such individuals are not powerless. They may stand out in their community as shining examples that other members aspire to. As such it is important to determine exactly what their characteristics are that negate the negative valuations that surround them. Where this is not possible the Implementation Group should realise that the activities of the empowerment project must not reinforce the stereotyping of the total community by unwittingly emphasising the powerlessness characteristics of some of its members, but instead must identify the range of strengths possessed by the community at large and use these when designing strategies.

If we now return to our question 'What is empowerment?' it should be clear that the concept of empowerment could be appropriate as a means of social intervention in any community where there is continuing, pervasive and systematic discrimination. Empowerment strategies deal with the particular blocks on problem-solving which stem from these impositions of external society or from the power-assertiveness of a small group within the community. In this context empowerment as a process refers to the design and growth of an effective support system for those members of the community who have been blocked from attaining a balance of power within the major social environments of their daily lives. This requires that individuals within the community should be helped to achieve their personal goals and to throw off the low self-esteem they experience as a result of the negative evaluations they are subject to. In so doing they become less vulnerable to bullies.

Strategies of Empowerment.

Empowerment strategies are generally aimed at improving problem-solving. Bloom (1975), writing two decades ago, has a fresh and interesting view of the similarities of different approaches to problem-solving taken by different professions. He shows that models of scientific problem-solving used by the different helping professions share a similar sequence despite their apparent dissimilarities. For example, task-centred casework, behaviour modification, client-centred group work, brief therapy and others may be seen as having seven basic stages from start to finish:

- orientation to problem-solving

- problem definition and formulation

- generation of alternatives regarding probable causes

- decision making

- implementation

- verification, and

- termination.

This general model of practice can be used to link the concept of empowerment to practice strategies.

Where the problems of a vulnerable community are defined by negative valuations held by either powerful group members or by the larger society around it then the first stage of the process proposed by Bloom, the orientation to problem solving, problem definition and formulation, has to cope with the specific responses the community makes to these negative evaluations. The empowerment activities in this stage have to be directed towards overcoming these specific responses before the client group is ready to consider the problem-solving process. Those members of the community who, in the context of bullying, may be defined as victims must first accept some of the responsibility for their plight. Once this step has been achieved it becomes more likely that the they will be prepared to engage in strategies that will ultimately improve the balance of power.

Subsequent stages in the empowerment process must deal with the removal of obstacles and the reinforcement of effective strategies evolved by the community members for problem-solving. As a result all empowerment activities should be structured so that they ensure the problem-solving process counteracts the negative valuations. Such activities generally have one or more of the following aims:

- helping the client group to perceive themselves as effective agents in achieving a problem solution.

- helping the client group to accept the practitioner as having knowledge and skills which can be transmitted to the client group for their own use.

- facilitating the client group to accept an equal partnership with the professional group in relation to the problem-solving effort.

- facilitating the client group to accept that the power imbalance is open to modification and that the problematic status quo can be overturned.

It can be seen, therefore, that the overall goal of the empowerment exercise is to help the client group that has been subjected to a systematic power imbalance resulting from pervasive negative evaluations to see themselves as a real force able to exert influence and so capable of bringing about a specific targeted effect. The need for the client group is to understand that they are using professionals as agents in effecting this change places an onus of responsibility on the Implementation Group. The group must ensure that community members know that, although they are being given help to resolve the problems of their powerlessness that this should not be taken to imply that they are the cause of their powerlessness.

Finally the design of the empowerment strategies must also take into account the organisational and bureaucratic processes that might themselves constitute blocks on the client group. It is often the case that the very agencies that are supposed to support and assist client groups function in such a way that they disempower those groups and leave them even more vulnerable to the negative evaluations of 'powerful' individuals or the larger society. The Implementation Group must, therefore, spend time considering the structure and strategies of delivery systems within the project that offer the greatest probability of facilitating empowerment.

Empowerment and a Community Anti-Bullying Project

This section focusses on the concept of empowerment as it relates to the impact of bullying within communities. As has already been stated bullying is a classic form of oppression and the negation of human rights. Victims and those who fear victimisation suffer a gross imbalance of power or perceived imbalance of poor. They also feel the embarrassment of shame arising from capitulating to the bullies; often people of their own kind, living in their own circumstances of housing, employment and social pressures, yet somehow able to exert an authority that they, the victims, lack. Many of these complex issues are revealed in the material that follows which frames the process of empowerment according to Bloom's (1975) headings. This material is drawn from my own work and so is derived from a particular community. Although there is likely to be much in common all communities show their own characteristics under these headings.

Problem Definition and Formulation: The Community and School Audits previously described have a central place under this heading. No work can justifiably done as problem definition unless these have been carried out correctly and the results collated and presented properly.

The following is a list of problems identified by the Community Audit of one project well known to the author.

Problem 1. 'The bullying around here is down to just a few people'.
Formulation: Two families from parallel streets are feuding. Their children carry on with the fights in school. Neighbours are 'tested out' to see if they are for or against each family. People who don't pass the test are intimidated or worse.
Problem 2. 'The bullies lie in wait and torment all of us'.
Formulation: The apartment blocks are linked by narrow sealed corridors with 'blind' right angle bends. Young men wait for victims to appear.
Problem 3: 'If these kids were brought up proper, they wouldn't go round doing what they do. It's the ones with the single Mums that are worst'.
Formulation: A high proportion of parents are single parent mothers with poor parenting skills. The influence of their children causes problems in the primary classes.

Generation of alternative explanation: The formulation above are plausible and no doubt at least partially correct. There are, however, alternative explanations and these can be helpful in establishing strategies.

Problem 1. Re-formulation: The family feud is a territory dispute over drug dealing but people are too frightened to inform the police.
Problem 2. Re-formulation: The young men have no jobs and no where else to go. The police won't allow them to stay on the streets so they spend some time in the corridors between the flats.
Problem 3. Re-formulation: Not only the single parents but many of those with partners believe in physical punishment which they use inconsistently. Many say they don't want to but don't know how to act differently.

We can see in these re-formulations the beginnings of problem solution strategies.

Decision making: By prioritising the different possibilities for each defined problem an Implementation Group can design appropriate remedial strategies for implementation.

> Problem 1. Strategy decision: The community police liaison officer will arrange surveillance of both families. The relevant members will be arrested, the remainder will be rehoused elsewhere at the instigation of the local housing officer on the Implementation Group.
>
> Problem 2. Strategy decision: The Youth Service and the Police will work together to establish youth activities on the outskirts of the estate. The employer representative will use his influence to increase youth training opportunities in the area.
>
> Problem 3. Strategic decision: An Under 5's club to be worked with self-help parenting skills being taught through the medium of play; 'parenting packs' to be used to stimulate this with parents playing a big part in their construction.

Following Bloom's structure, the stages of Implementation and Verification (Monitoring) will take place in accordance with strategic plans drawn up between the Implementation and Monitoring groups. Termination occurs naturally when the community takes full ownership of the new arrangements for Problems 2 and 3 and any subsequent reoccurrence if difficulties of the same type as Problem 1.

CHAPTER 7

Using the local media

In chapter three the idea was introduced that popular local media would be a powerful force for conveying the intentions of the project and the information it makes available to members of the targeted community. The Implementation Group will be only too aware of the power of the media to convey attitudes, impressions and facts to local people. Indeed, there has been a massive use of the media for transmitting health related information to the general public from the late 1960s onwards, television viewers have been exposed to the effects of smoking, overeating, alcohol abuse, AIDS and a host of other serious issues. If only a small proportion of viewers or readers take up and utilise the information then the purpose will have been well served (eg. Flora and Wallack, 1990)

Yet the media is not just a powerful force for the transmission of useful information, it may also be a powerful force for the transmission of faulty information, inappropriate attitudes and dangerous role models for social behaviour (eg. Paik and Comstock, 1994) and this is of great concern to many professional groups (eg. Lazar, 1994). There appears to be a direct link between media material and aggression. The Implementation Group cannot ignore the possiblity that if, for example, it was to release information about specific types of bullying or the problems of particular victims this may be seized upon by people, particularly young people, as an example for their own behaviour. As a result there may be an accusation that, far from helping, the Implementation Group has simply put ideas in the minds of would-be bullies.

The temptation is to say that the good done by the transmission of information through the local media will out-weigh whatever bad may be done. The Implementation Group must, however, be aware that there is a direct link between the mass media and the social fabric. McIlwraith (1987) reviews literature showing that children's violence can be influenced through television, as can the nature and type of suicides and even the general publics' perception of crime seriousness (See Appendix A). It is vital that the Implementation Group presents its information in such a way to refute accusations of glorification of bullying. This chapter now examines the use of media and provides a guide to the Implementation Group.

General Trends in the Use of Local Media

There has been a long debate within the public health sector with the gurus of communication and media theory about the effectiveness of the local and mass media in promoting healthy behaviours (eg McGuire, 1984, Flora and Wallock, 1990). In general a review of the relevant literature shows that there is significant media use in promoting both physical and mental health. There are concerns, however, that this usage does not fully exploit the power of the media and that the aims and objectives are excessively limited. Flora and Wallock (1990) conducted a survey in California and concluded that although over 95% of health professionals acknowledged the power of the media and nearly as many were interested in using the media, in practice there was significant under-use and a restricted set of aims. It is useful to examine some of the difficulties that Flora and Wallock exposed in the context of mental health and the media. Many of their points may guide media use in respect of bullying.

Firstly they found that there was a generally low level of objectives set by health professionals for use of the media and that these were concerned primarily with increasing awareness about various health problems. There was seldom any significant follow up of effectiveness.

The next most common usage was described by Flora and Wallock as 'supplementation activities' and which they characterised as public relations events (such as press conferences) having little to do with efforts to change behaviour in relation to whatever health problem was targetted. Next, there was interest in using the media to simply get information into homes or places of work. Although a valuable goal it does not reflect a serious attempt to involve the media in a partnership towards long term goals about behaviour-change. Not surprisingly, hardly any attempts were found to evaluate the value of such media usage.

It is probable that these limitations are not due to the inability of the media to do more but to a restricted promotion-oriented concept of media usage held by health professionals. This effectively precluded the media representation of vital behaviour-change activities needed by communities to evolve their new awareness into sensible patterns of responding. The Implementation Group should guard against such limitations.

The reasons for this limited media usage also have much to do with the size of budgets. An advertising campaign is a very expensive process. To some extent this can be overcome by forming an effective partnership with representatives of the local media who might be able to offer an at-cost or even free service if their own organisation can benefit from association with the campaign. A more immediate reason is that the professionals who mount campaigns of this sort seldom have media expertise. Only a few health professionals are aware that there is support in the literature for using the media to initiate healthful behaviour change. The paper by Flora and Wallock reviews several sources of evidence up to the late 1980s which demonstrate conclusively that effective media programmes can bring about significant changes in community behaviour to diminish health risks. Such effects are found over a wide range of health problems and it is useful to be able to demonstrate this diversity to the Implementation Group. Thus, Levy and Stokes (1987) were able to demonstrate a change in peoples fibre intake in breakfast cereals as a consequence of a media campaign and Katcher (1987) was able to demonstrate that the frequency of scalding through dangerous use hot tap water was also reduced as a consequence of a effective mass media campaign. Flay (1987) was able to demonstrate that a long term mass media anti-smoking programme formed a useful part of the activities leading to a reduction in smoking.

Given this evidence there is reason to believe that mass and local media representation of anti-bullying projects can be helpful in a number of vital areas. These include:

- raising funds

- raising the profile of the project

- recruiting paid staff or volunteers

- promoting the policy of the programme

- changing the behaviour of people in the community in respect of both bullies and victims

- slowly modifying attitudes, particularly to victims

- raising awareness of the project and transmitting information within the community.

Although television is the most powerful media of all because of its reach across social strata and mass appeal, it is as important to use radio and newspaper, and to delineate media type appropriately. Thus although the small time-bites that anti-bullying projects will command on local television may not convey much information, they certainly direct community members to more detailed information in newspapers, local magazines and local radio. The inter-relationship or the different media types should be carefully thought through for each 'message' the Implementation Group wishes to bring to the attention of community members.

Examples of Media Usage

The following examples are of TV, radio and newspaper treatment that have been of value to projects the writer has been involved with. Each has played a part in meeting the aims listed above.

Television: Inclusion of local news programmes; length up to 2 minutes and made up of interviews with a primary school headteacher on bullying outside school, interviews with an adolescent victim, scenes of local bullying 'hot spots'.

Television: Taking part in a small 'expert group' debate on bullying.

Radio: 'Phone-in' on bullying.

Radio: Interview about bullying in general.

Radio: Interviews about serious bullying incidents that have led to well-publicised suicides.

Radio: Interviews about bullying in schools.

Radio: Interviews about bullying in the community.

Radio: Fund raising.

Newspapers: These are divided into two groups; news features written by in-house journalists, and editorial features submitted by project staff.

News features cover bullying incidents and are also good for fund raising. Editorial features are vital for awareness raising and information gaining. Two successful pieces are shown below. The first preceded a programme to engage parents and playgroup staff in 'socialisation' activities across the area targeted. It 'spearheaded' a series of promotional activities that led to parents and workers understand their key role in helping very young children learn better strategies than those based on aggression for interacting with their peers. This article was carried in an influential newspaper and attracted a great deal of interest, not only from the preschool sector but also from funding agents.

The Tiny Bullies

The distraught young mother gathered her little child to her, gently holding his head and hugging him. They were both weeping and she wiped his streaming face delicately as she tried to find the words to describe what had happened to him.

Eventually we were able to piece together her distressing story. He was being bullied. Not by the bullies of our stereotypes, hulking ominous brutes with cold sneers and coarse laughter, but by other five-year olds, infants just like himself. Only nastier.

It still seems incredible to us who work daily with victims and bullies that this vile behaviour should be present in children so young.

This little child was totally unremarkable. He wasn't 'posh', often a red rag to the ignorant. He didn't wear glasses or a hearing aid, the badges of disability that attract the attentions of the more fortunate and he didn't smell. He was just an ordinary little boy to all except his mother who adored him.

So why was he singled out for weeks of being kicked and punched, his little toys snatched away from him and broken? Why did such young children wait carefully until teachers' backs were turned and a sufficient melee of children had gathered to hide their actions, assemble their alibis and otherwise premeditate their crimes against him?

Perhaps he was rude to them, maybe he wouldn't share or looked down his nose at their games — all common reasons for this mobbing behaviour? Maybe, as people are wont to say, 'He brought it on himself'?

None of these. It was simply that his young mother was crippled with cerebral palsy and her neighbours talked disparagingly in front of their children about 'that spas down the road' as they watched her limp to the shops. Maybe that's why the little boy, whose existence, lovely presentation and gentle ways represented her conquest of disability, became a victim. A victim of other little children who acted out the ignorant and dangerous attitudes of their parents, people who lacked the intellect and the humanity to recognise her achievements and value them.

At one time the received wisdom told us that children under the age of six to seven couldn't really be classed as bullies. This view was reasonable because, it was thought, to be a bully you had to appreciate that it was alright to inflict pain on someone else provided that you didn't get caught. Infants were not supposed to have the understanding of social behaviour to premeditate behaviours to this extent. So their aggression was seen as impulsive rather than calculated, driven by anger rather than a desire to hurt.

Our experiences indicate that this view is no longer correct. Some young children are capable of planning 'to get' someone and they are more likely to do so when in the company of others just like them. Their skills in this area are quite refined. One young bully told us that he and his friends knew exactly when was the best time to make another child cry — it was when the victim needed to go to the toilet. If the bullies could stop him going by being in the toilets ahead of him then he would sob and wet himself, much to the annoyance of the class teacher. This little victim eventually refused to go to school and is even now, three weeks later, unable to talk about school without tears.

Such cunning comes from somewhere; children aren't born with it. It is like any other skill, it develops and is refined by practice. Since schools don't have it on the curriculum it is likely that it comes from within the home or the surroundings of the home. That's why we keeping saying that schools don't create bullies, they just import them. Listening to some little bullies talk, particularly when they are expressing angry feelings, we hear adult words and phrases and know that these children are mimics rather than originators.

As far as child rearing is concerned we only get out what we put in. So gentle kind parents tend to have gentle kind children. Angry aggressive parents tend to send aggressive children to school taking with them the patterns of hostility and dismissive attitudes of their mentors. The proof of this pudding often comes when the parents of victims confront those of the bullies only to find themselves being abused in one way or another.

That's exactly what happened to the young mother we started with. She went to talk to the mother of one of her little son's persecutors outside the school gates. The abuse she was met with confirmed that the bully was merely the faithful acolyte of the mother, an automaton programmed to hate.

We are often told proudly by the parents of bullies that it is a tough world and they are glad their children can stand on their own two feet. In so doing they make the tragic errors of confusing assertiveness with aggression and of mistaking coercion for negotiation. Their passive acceptance of their child's behaviour acts as a consent for its continuation and refinement.

Perhaps they should understand what the future may hold for their young children. One survey showed that children who were aggressive at the age of three to four then they were still likely to be so at age eight. Another revealed that many young adults with criminal records of violence had histories of aggression going back to the age of eight. If these findings are put together it is clear that many infant bullies of today may be the jail bait of tomorrow.

That's not all, the personalities that some bullies develop go against them in other ways. Poor employment prospects, failed marriages, alcohol abuse and personal dissatisfaction are common amongst them. It seems that no-one does well out of bullying in the end.

Bullying may not seem like much of a problem to those of us whose children are neither victims nor bullies. But think of this, one child in six will be bullied today, tomorrow — every day. Perhaps they will be scarred for life by the experience. Maybe their parents are powerless to help them against the power of the bullies' own parents. Maybe they need us to stand up for them and make the community response that is required to stop bullying for all our sakes.

The second article shown here was run by a large tabloid style Sunday paper and was used to trigger interest in adult bullying experienced nationally and more particularly within the community area of the project. Once again it was highly successful and led not only to adult victims coming forward but also to much successful discussion between trade unions and local employers.

Workplace Bullying (An article in three parts)

It's Sunday evening and Cathy Moore is starting to get edgy. She can hardly eat her tea and snaps at the kids. Her stomach starts to churn and by nine o'clock she has been sick. Her sleep that night is fitful and her head aches from the permanent frown she wears. Monday morning finds her weeping in the bathroom. Any excuse, any at all, would be enough to keep her from going to work. Why should she go? Surely the money isn't worth the scorn, insults and foul language her boss heaps upon her. What can she do about it, no-one would believe her?

Workplace bullying is a vast problem for this country, each day it keeps thousands away from work and heaps up endless domestic problems with the frustrations it causes. The forms it takes are beyond counting yet the reasons for it often boil down to just one.

Envy.

Not envy of things or skills but generally of some quality that the bullies do not possess and which they feel is a challenge to them or their position. Over the years that we have worked with both bullies and victims we have discovered how varied the nature of this envy can be. Good looks, happiness, popularity, a keen brain — anything that the bully thinks of as being a threat.

The activities of the bully are invariably secretive. Just like child bullies so adult bullies make sure that they are not caught in the act. They may not use physical aggression or scream loud abuse at their targets, instead they use criticism, derision, Chinese whispers and other insidious behaviour to bewilder and intimidate their victims.

On first glance none of these behaviours sound bad enough to drive people like Cathy to the point of a nervous breakdown. Yet the sheer grinding persistence of them can wear down the strongest personality. In the end victims may feel that they are useless and not up to the job. Their self-esteem is at rock bottom and they feel powerless to fight back.

Cathy went that way. She did have a breakdown and eventually lost the job she desperately needed. Her bullying boss rubbed salt into her wounds and sent her a letter saying how sorry he was to lose her.

Second Part: WHAT MAKES A BULLY?

Robert Taylor is a self-confessed workplace bully. He has a middle management position in the food distribution industry with about forty people working to him. 'I've always been a bully, even during my days at secondary school. A lot of it has to do with the violent upbringing I had at my father's hands — he used to beat me and I would take it out of someone at school. He did more than that though. He used to set about me with his tongue as well — I couldn't do anything right. The funny thing was that people outside our family thought he was a wonderful charitable man. Well, they certainly didn't know him! One thing he did teach me, though, was to make sure that no-one ever got the better of me. I make sure they still don't'.

Robert is one of thousands of workplace bullies who are what they are because of their own violent and verbally aggressive upbringings. Most of them were bullies during their school days as well.

Winny Blake is another bully who has reluctantly come to acknowledge what she has done to people. 'My problem was that I only knew one way to get things done. When I was made a supervisor I found that making the women afraid of me was the best way for me to earn the bonuses that went with the job'. She had to supervise a line of about sixteen women who packed electrical components. Without training in people management she fell back on the strategies that her elder sisters had with her — they used threats and scorn to get things done.

Like so many people in her position Winny used fear where she should have used discussion and encouragement. But in doing so she also got back at her abusive sisters from years previously.

Many workplace bullies are like Winny, they discover that the kind of hostility used against them in the past can help them in the present. Unfortunately they are so successful at getting high rates of work from their staff that their own bosses often turn a blind eye to their methods.

Third Part: WHAT MAKES A VICTIM

No matter how long we work with bullies and their victims we never seem to get used to the terrifying levels of rage, pain, fear, jealousy and self-doubt that surfaces when finally someone blows the whistle on workplace bullying.

The first reaction of most victims is astonishment: 'How can this be happening to me?'. They are bullied for no apparent reason that has anything to do with them as individuals — the problem lies entirely within the bully.

For some, however, there is no astonishment — what happens to them at work is only an extension of what happened to them at home or at school. It is another aspect of the long term problems they have had with relationships — problems that have raised the label VICTIM above their heads in neon lights.

Simon was one of these. 'After long sessions of counselling I realise that I never could relate well to people. My mother was obsessed with me, she dominated me with love and never let me depart from her ideal view of what I should be like. When finally I escaped her into school or work then it was only to find that I didn't know how to get on with people. I almost used to invite them to bully me in order to gain their attention. Well, now it's become a habit'.

Jan Thomson knows she is another sort of victim. 'I don't have many happy memories of childhood. I always seemed to be trying to get between my Mum and Dad. They argued incessantly about anything and everything. I couldn't stand it and took it upon myself to try and appease them. All that got me was a lot of hostility from them both. They taught me that I was just an annoying little girl who they couldn't love. Instead they gave their affection to my younger brother when he came along. I was out of their family even though I was still living under their roof'.

Jan's story of angry rejecting parents is not uncommon amongst people who become victims. They learn to be submissive in order to try and avoid further confrontation and rejection.

Unfortunately a submissive person is exactly what a bully needs.

(Pete Randall is Project Director of the North Hull Anti-Bullying Project and Mike Donohue is Project Co-ordinator. The project hotline is 0482 858585).

Notice how the last article gives the project hotline number. This is vital for publicity but it does lead to a spate of self-referrals that the Implementation Group must prepare for.

TV and video portrayal of violence is very important to an anti community project. Many parents will ask for guidance about it and will have concerns that their children are being badly influenced by w... they see in cartoons and allegedly family viewing. Other parents may not understand that children and adolescents are influenced by what they watch; they need information to help them understand that they have a key role in the extent to which young people are affected. The present state of knowledge is summarised in the following handout for parents. It was prepared as part of the writer's own Community Anti-Bullying project and can be reproduced in a more suitable form (mention made of specific research studies are fully referenced in the References section):-

Television Violence: Effects on Children and Young People
by Pete Randall

Several years ago a very distressed mother entered my office. She was in tears and had difficulty getting out her story. Her son was being bullied. Badly bullied.

There was nothing strange for me in that, bullying was an all too common problem, even then. What made this unusual was the manner of the bullying. The children involved were only eight and nine year olds and their hero was David Carradine.

This was at the time when that actor was bringing Kung Fu to the Western world. Children and young adolescents were lapping it up. Just about every other free-writing exercise in primary schools turned up tales of Kung Fu. David Carradine was to that generation what Roy Rogers had been to me.

Unfortunately what stuck with the children was the stylised violence. None of the programme's synthetic Confucian-type philosophy with its candles, bald monks and morality made any impact on them at all. David Carradine was providing a strong role model for violence and it was attractively packaged.

It shouldn't have surprised me to find that the small victim his tear-streaked mum described was nothing more than a kick bag for the little Kung Fu thugs. I was, however, surprised by the faithful mimicking that the little bullies had used and been so serious about. From that time on I have been aware of the 'fads' of violence that follow TV and film characters. That's what this article is all about.

As parents we must all have wondered about the effect TV has on our children. We know that it must influence them in some way because it is such a big part of their lives. Even at school it figures in the curriculum and on special occasions when teachers allow videos to be screened. As I watch my five-year old's reactions to the violence and sex that creeps unwanted into family viewing time I am both pleased and frightened. Pleased that he seems to have no adverse reaction, frightened that he doesn't. On the one hand I don't want him to be affected by it, on the other I don't want him to be brutalised into accepting it as normal.

Now Christmas is approaching. The television will bring its usual seasonal mixed messages for children. There will be films about reindeer doing grand things to get presents to small children and there will be others showing gratuitous violence. As far as television goes Christmas is always a scary time for me because there is such a concentration of good guys doing the most horrendous things to the bad guys and getting praised for it. Just what does this say to children?

I'll come back to that point a bit later but for now let's just review what is suspected about TV violence.

For a start there is a conflict of opinion about the effects it has on people. There are those who believe that there is a direct link between what is screened and young people's behaviour. The mother I opened with would definitely agree with that. Then there are those who say there is no link at all, or at least none that can be proven. Then there are people like me who say that it is probably a great deal more complex than either simple belief, something in between where some young people are affected by it and many aren't.

One very influential report said that TV violence was definitely associated with the aggression of children and young people. This was commissioned by the Surgeon General of the United States. It was followed up by an equally persuasive report by the American National Institute of Mental Health in 1982. Both reports concluded that there was sufficient evidence to justify the conclusion that televised violence is a contributory cause of children's violence. Not long after Karate films became very popular in this country and I for one witnessed a spate of severe Bruce Lee type bullying incidents.

But there were many who disagreed and published their views that these reports had not been properly carried out. The most influential appeared late in 1982 and was commissioned by the National Broadcasting Company of America. I am sure you can see some similarities here with the no-smoking campaign of the eighties. On the one hand the public health bodies were saying 'It's bad for you, give it up'; on the other the main producing industry was saying 'Nothing is proved one way or another so keep right on watching what you enjoy'.

One important study went further than some of the simple research and actually looked at figures for criminal violence across America. The overall conclusion was that there was no relationship between the amount of television watched and the amount of such crime. In fact the reverse was true, the greater the amount of television the lower was the violent crime rate. One of the psychologists involved, Steven Messner (1986), went so far as to suggest that this was because people at home watching television couldn't be out on the streets harming others.

Well, it all makes work for the researchers to do but what do we make of it as responsible parents? In my opinion the best thing to believe is that some children are affected and some aren't. There is good evidence to support this view. For example, Wendy Josephson (1987), a social psychologist, found that boys who watched an exciting violent film clip were more likely to act aggressively in a game of hockey afterwards than those who simply watched an exciting car chase. The boys who were most affected were those who were rated by their teachers as being characteristically aggressive anyway. In other words the children who were already aggressive by nature were the ones that were most influenced by the violence that they witnessed.

This is a highly important finding because it would explain why different people have discovered extremely variable results. Depending on the nature of the children they 'tested' they would have found no effect on some but a significant one on others.

But there is more to it than just the natural temperaments of children. Two psychologists, Kim Walker and Donald Marley (1991), studied the effect of TV violence on adolescents. They found that there was an effect on behaviour but it wasn't a simple one. The crucial factor was not the amount of violence watched or the severity of it. Instead the important factor was whether or not the young people actually liked the violence. If they did they were far more likely to be aggressive after watching it.

Parental factors were also important. The degree of aggressiveness following exposure to violence on TV was influenced by the acceptance of it by parents. Their opinions could reduce the effect on their youngsters although how this works is not yet entirely clear.

These findings fit closely with my own experiences of the families I have met where screen violence has been an issue. Take this one.

Clive was ten when he was arrested for assault. He was the leader of a small gang of younger boys who had watched three violent videos in succession. They had been given them to watch by his mother. She had wanted them kept quiet and entertained whilst she went shopping with her husband for the day. Clive and his gang had left the house when the last film ended and seriously assaulted two younger children. The attack took place in a park at six o'clock in the evening. When asked why he had done it Clive was confused. The children had been cheeky to him and he was just sticking up for his rights as he had seen the good guys on the films do. Part of his reasoning was that if his mother had encouraged him to watch the violence then surely it couldn't be all that wrong.

You may think that Clive must be a very unintelligent child to mistake the violence he had watched with real life situations. In fact he was a boy of average ability and his confusion was genuine. Why then should the TV violence have affected him in this way?

Studies of aggression in children throw some light on to this puzzle. Repeated exposure to TV violence, particularly where the 'good guys' are violent and get praised for their heroic aggression, creates, over a period of time, an association between the reasons for the fictional violence and every day frustrations. In effect a child begins to 'store' the idea of particularly aggressive actions alongside memories of familiar situations that are frustrating.

Psychologists call stored patterns 'algorithms' and we use them for all sorts of every day activities where predictable events occur and we need to make a similar response each time. For example, the bed-side alarm goes off and is a trigger for us to embark on a large set of behaviours which end up with us getting to work. The pattern is repeated in a similar way every day and we go through it on auto-pilot.

The algorithms for aggression in young children are formed because of the repeated exposure they get to powerful role models who show them how to change things their way through the use of violence. No wonder that children who are already easily frustrated are so readily influenced by what they see continually. And no wonder that one psychologist, Harry Hoberman (1990), has argued that the media should stigmatise any actor who repeatedly portrays violent characters. He goes on to suggest that parents should be educated in the ways that they should modify their children's viewing habits so that they don't seem to condone violence.

It is clear then that some children will be affected by television violence again this Christmas as they are every other day of the year. These children will mostly be boys who are easily upset or frustrated. They need responsible parenting which may turn off the violence or at least explain it in terms of real life. Without that kind of guidance some will end up like Clive.

CHAPTER 8

The counselling and telecounselling service

The community project must be more than an effort to weaken the antecedents for bullying in the targeted area. Although that is a worthy goal and will ultimately serve individuals well it does nothing for those who are already victims or bullies. This chapter deals with the establishment of a service designed to help those who are already badly affected by bullying and who need support as they endeavour to resolve their problems.

Many victims of bullying need some sensible and direct advice about what to do about it. Parents particularly can respond well to a 'quick fix' of tips for alleviating the victimisation of their children. Some strategies are given in Chapter 9 and little more is needed than relaying these to parents and monitoring the results.

Other clients, however, require more support. They need not only the strategies but also a process of personal empowerment to help them develop the confidence to move forward successfully. Such clients need counselling and this chapter provides basic information needed to develop successful counselling within the project team.

Certain assumptions are made here:

• there is a willingness on the part of at least some project group members or volunteers to support victims,

- these people are not trained counsellors but have the qualities of empathy and social understanding upon which counselling skills may be developed,

- there is no time for these 'counsellors' to see clients regularly over a very long period of time so that a task-centred approach should be the main 'style' of the service offered, and that there is a network of professional services available for onward referral of those clients who cannot be helped by this approach,

- there are comfortable facilities available for regular counselling sessions,

- that telephone counselling is available as part of a hot-line service, and that regular clinical supervision is available from at least one experienced and professionally qualified counsellor to ensure that a quality service is maintained.

The details surrounding these assumptions and the processes they require are given in the following sections.

Ethical Considerations

All personal services requiring interventions on the part of clients experiencing psychological or social difficulties should be delivered within an ethical framework. The counselling services should work to the Code of Practice specified by the British Association for Counselling but there may be other methods of intervention that do not fit. The following guidelines are sufficiently robust to cover the whole project and safeguard its clients:

(1) Project workers should always endeavour to use procedures which are in the best interests of their client or clients, minimising risk and maximising benefits over both the short and long term, while also safeguarding against possible harmful effects to others or the community as a whole.

(2) Choice and style of intervention should always be justified by the available evidence, taking into account possible alternatives or styles of work, the degree of demonstrated efficacy, and the time and cost of alternative intervention.

(3) Project workers should make every attempt to discuss and negotiate the goals and methods of intervention with the client, family and

group. These may have to be renegotiated from time to time, or intervention terminated.

(4) In situations where consent is impossible to obtain, the worker may not always be able to fulfil these criteria. These situations may include work with, for example, very young children and some clients with learning difficulties. In these situations consent should be obtained from the primary caregiver or those with parental responsibility.

(5) It is vital to the project worker's approach and to the project as a whole that he or she plans and implements all intervention in such a way as to allow its effectivess to be evaluated.

(6) Project workers should continually reappraise their competence both from formal training and from their experience. If they are faced with a situation in which his or her level of skill is in doubt, they should immediately seek help from their line manager.

(7) The project workers should avail themselves of opportunities provided by the project to up-date their knowledge and skills.

Counselling the Victims of Bullying

Counsellors working for an anti-bullying project must be aware of the special issues that the victims of bullying face and learn when to seek the help of professionals from other agencies. For example, bullying that is associated with the alcohol abuse of a particular family member may result in a need for a victim to seek counselling support but resolution of the core problem can only come from alleviating the reasons for the alcohol abuse. That generally takes a specialist and the project counsellors must know where to refer to.

Counselling within an anti-bullying project is best suited to cases where the clients are regular victims of bullies whose activities could eventually be countered by the clients themselves. The whole project is about empowerment, this aspect of it is merely the extension of the concept of community empowerment to the individual. The main aim must be to enskill and enable the clients to use effective strategies to stop themselves being victimised. The aim must not be to fight the clients' battles for them or to allow them to manipulate project counsellors into becoming their advocates. It is necessary, however, to consider the particular difficulties that victims have which make them a rather specialised type of client.

The characteristics of victims have already been discussed and from these is derived a list of special features that the project counsellors should be aware of.

Adult Victims

The following items relate to adult victims or to the parents of child victims:

- a deep sense of shock ('Why is this happening to me/us?');

- a sense of failure ('Why couldn't I stop it for myself?');

- a feeling of being impotent ('I must be a weak person to let this happen to me/my child');

- low self-esteem ('I must be pretty worthless if people want to do this to me'), and

- a fear about future relationships ('no-one will want to know a weak person like me').

Not all victims will articulate all of these concerns but many will experience some if not most of them. Their effect is to disempower the clients by blocking the development of more adaptive constructs. The counsellors' main task is to help the victims replace these constructs with effective forward thinking.

Although adult victims may have comparable experiences, that does not mean they will all react in the same way. Tyhurst (1951) describes three patterns of reaction:

1. Disturbed behaviour, such as confusion or disorientation or being paralysed by fear (10-25% of victims).

2. Stunning or bewilderment (approximately 75%) such that awareness of what is happening is poor and perhaps there is only a weak understanding of their emotions despite a physiological fear/stress reaction.

3. Controlled behaviour designed to reduce the effects of trauma (10 to 25% of victims) where the victims are fully aware and react sensibly. These victims may still need counselling to help them ventilate their emotions.

Child Victims

Child victims have different issues to confront:

- A poor understanding of what is happening to them beyond the immediate physical or psychological assaults,

- Escape reactions which might be counterproductive in other ways (e.g. truancy, bribing bullies to leave them alone, feigning illness to avoid school, lying),

- Sometimes an ambivalent attitude to the bully ('I know he hurts me but I still want to be his friend'),

- For some, a sense of inevitability ('He's bullied so many in my class, it's just my turn now'), and

- For others, a hatred for adults who fail to protect them.

As with adults, not all child victims will show all or even some of these responses; many will simply want the bullying stopped and manage to keep an accurate sense of perspective as to where it fits into their lives. This does not mean, however, that they are not deeply hurt and terrified by the bullying or that they don't need help in dealing with these feelings. It does mean that at this time at least their self-esteem and self-respect has not been irrevocably damaged.

Awareness

Many clients who are or have been on the receiving end of bullying feel helpless with regard to overcoming that situation. Somehow they must become aware that the problem of bullying, be it psychological or physical, becomes more of a threat if they give it unduly personal significance. Victims must become aware that they need not, should not and must not experience shame or feel that they are the only ones to experience bullying. With that must come an acknowledgement that they have not been diminished in any way as worthwhile people by the unpleasant experiences.

The awareness raising process of counselling should not stop when these issues are acknowledged by clients. They must also become aware of the primary requirement that they must take responsibility for facing up to and rejecting the aggression that bullies may continue to inflict upon them. A golden rule for counselling victims of bullying should be that a victim stays a victim as long as he or she accepts the passive role. Should the client keep asking 'How can I cope with this?', the counsellor must reply so that the client becomes aware that 'coping with' is merely a restatement of the passive role. It implies acceptance and a lack of assertiveness in dealing with the bullying at a more proactive level. This awareness is 'the foundation on which you (the client) can begin to rebuild your battered self-esteem and eventually learn how to prevent the nightmare from recurring' (Crawford, 1985).

Assertiveness

Some people confuse assertiveness with aggression. They find it difficult to conceptualise that an individual can insist on their basic human rights and refuse to accept a restriction of those rights without being aggressive. It is probably this that causes some parents to appear to support their children as bullies (Hall, 1995). They feel that the best way to survive in a tough world is by being tough and see bullying not so much as an assault upon others but a means of establishing dominance and the right to obtain and enjoy whatever resources may be available. Some theologians (e.g. Katz and Blundy, 1994) have argued that our society has seen a considerable shift in recent times towards a paradigm of individuality where the traditional values of mutual dependency, reciprocated care and concern of others and the provision of service to the community has been replaced by a far more self-centred and self-supportive ethos. In claiming that the importance of family has been much diminished over the years some theologians, sociologists and politicians have come to believe their own propaganda whereas the true evidence is that family ethos is still alive and well throughout the western world (eg. Richards, 1995). The media continues to suggest that the traditional values of relationships have been abandoned but at the same time peoples' needs for security and roots continue. Against this background, some writers speak of assertiveness as a vital component in a new 'self-centred' culture; as part of the personal growth movement which all individuals striving for self-development must obtain and utilise.

Although some of the explanations are inadequate and do not readily fit the facts that individuals still strive towards cohesive family existence and that communities based on families continue to thrive, it is correct that nonassertive behaviour is strongly correlated with low self-esteem (Back and Back, 1991). It is also related to a lack of respect for oneself and a maladaptive desire to always appease, please and gratify other people. The fear of confrontation that is implicit within such behaviour is strongly associated with anxiety and is a common antecedent for victim status (Adams, 1992).

Whereas nonassertive behaviour is associated with low self-esteem it is also true that aggressive behaviour is fundamentally manipulative in that it involves trying to control and get the better of other people. It is a crude form of manipulation and a lack of respect for other people and a refusal to acknowledge or meet their needs is implicit. Whether in child or adult bullying, such regular aggressive behaviours are reinforced by the submissiveness of victims and personal ego-gratification.

Simplistically, it is assumed that assertiveness is in some way a healthy mid-point between these two extremes (e.g. Luzio-Lockett, 1995). Definitions of assertiveness also imply such a balance. For example Back and Back (1991) believe that assertiveness is aimed at standing up for one's own rights in such a way that the rights of other people are not violated. 'Expressing your needs, wants, opinions, feeling and beliefs in direct, honest and appropriate ways' (Back and Back, 1991, p. 1) is offered as the working definition. It fails to take into account that often, in standing up for our own rights we actually confront and affront others who want something different from us. Thus, a neighbour who wishes to mow his lawn on Sunday has the right to do so but, in so doing, he may affront the man next door who believes that Sunday is a sacred day. The man with the mower will claim that he is merely asserting his rights while the man next door may feel that he is the victim of an aggressive act. It not possible to be assertive without being perceived to be aggressive some of the time. Counsellors of victims must help their clients understand that their newfound assertiveness may lead to fresh confrontations.

Other simplistic analyses of assertiveness suggest that it implies open, direct and honest communications which, in turn, enable other people to respond in an equally open and direct way. Yet it is well known that many people do not feel comfortable with openness and directness, they prefer the telling of 'little white lies' to protect other people and to prevent confrontations. It is a mistake to always believe that nonassertive behaviour is an act of cowardice and the result of poor self-esteem.

One implication of assertiveness does, however, have much to do with the benefits of counselling given to victim clients. Assertiveness is also about regaining control and empowerment to take back whatever valuable feelings of confidence, beliefs in oneself and positive self-constructs that faulty socialisation processes and bullying behaviour have taken away. In many ways this provides a better counselling goal for many victims. It does not say to these victims that they must modify the bullies' behaviour; instead it requires the victims to take control of their own behaviour and remove from it those aspects which mark them out as targets of victimisation.

Many adults may respond to such overtures from the counsellor by pointing out that the people doing the bullying are, for example, their bosses who may be abusing their authority but are nevertheless in a position of power. 'What can we do about him, he is our boss?', is a frequent excuse given for the submissive and placatory behaviour that victims often demonstrate in the context of work place harassment. Even where there are effective work place equal opportunities and anti-harassment policies in operation, such clients often fail to engage the right procedures to make their plight known. They accept it rather than tackle it. It seems that the key to this variety of non-assertive behaviour lies in mastering appropriate skills and techniques which are associated with the client beginning to judge his or her own performance independently of the resulting behaviour from the bully or, indeed, from the outcome of the interaction (Guirdham, 1990).

The beginnings of such adaptive behaviour actually lie in the use of the word 'I'. The client must be empowered to say, for example, 'I think that...', 'I want to...'; this is the first way forward in taking ownership of the client's own feelings, opinions and attitudes without attempting to embed them weakly in placating remarks. It is often the case that the ways clients express themselves are long winded and roundabout, lacking a clear message. A simple but gradual movement towards clarity and brevity will create an impression in the minds of the bullies that this person is unlikely to submit to their aggressive manipulation.

Some strategies for assertiveness training are given in chapter 9.

THE COUNSELLING SERVICE

The Task Centred Approach

The task-centred approach is founded on the concept that small successes are reinforcing and build confidence and self-esteem, and that people are more likely to be empowered and to achieve these successes if they are actively pursuing a goal they have chosen. Task-centred counselling is designed to assist people make choices about what they want to do and then help them locate the necessary resources, both internal and external, for doing it. In taking this approach counsellors must acccept that, for the most part, clients are reasoning people who are best acquainted with their problems and therefore the best ones to set the goals for change.

Right at the core of the task-centred approach are the concepts central to the community anti-bullying project, namely **partnership** and **empowerment.** With regard to partnership, the task-centred approach accepts that the professional counsellor may be the best assessor of problems and may have professional skills in the resolution of those problems. But, the fact remains that the clients themselves are the best acquainted with their difficulties and circumstances under which they can be resolved. The concept of empowerment has already been discussed and as this section of the chapter proceeds the reader should see how the task-centred approach is a genuine strategy to facilitate it.

The task-centred approach is well known to councellors and dates back to the mid 1960s. At one time it was thought that the task-centred approach would not be as adequate in resolving difficulties as much more extended casework (e.g. Reid and Shyne, 1969). For the majority of clients there is little difference between the briefer approach of task-centred practice and more extended non-directive approaches. In respect of social work, Reid and Epstein (1972) developed a model of social work practice which extolled the benefits of shorter time limits in intervention. Their systematic model introduced the notion of **tasks** as central to the process of empowering clients and from that time onwards the task-centred approach has become a very powerful model for intervention. There have been numerous research and social work publications about it and these are reviewed by Doel and Marsh (1992) for those who wish to pursue the background to this approach in greater depth than is possible here.

The Task-Centred Approach in Action

After a period of preparation and before evaluation of the intervention there are three basic sequences in task-centred work.

Preparation: The preparatory stage, sometimes called the mandate for intervention, is the period where the counsellor finds out from the client why the work is necessary. The mandate questions the justification for intervening and, if there is no satisfactory answer to that question, then it is not wise for any intervention to proceed. For example, an alleged victim who seeks counselling as a guise for inveigling the project workers into functioning as an advocate against an alleged bully or even an organisation may be told that their difficulties do not fall in the remit of the project. Perhaps they need a solicitors' letter or some other response which is outwith the aims and objectives of the project. Such disputes are commonly brought to community projects and generally involve matters, such as boundary disputes about fences or noise levels, where one neighbour is seeking assistance to get another neighbour into trouble or to limit their own rights. The mandate for intervention has to be clearly established otherwise both counsellor and client may be working to different objectives and confusion and further pain will result.

Stage One: Exploring the Problems

The counsellors role in this first stage begins by encouraging the clients to present their difficulties using a broad brush approach. What is required is an overall picture of the difficulties that are being experienced. Though bullying may be the label that the client is giving for contacting the service it may well be that a host of other problems are as serious. These commonly include financial worries, concerns about physical resources, worries about relationships within the family or anxieties about child management and upbringing. Counsellors should resist the temptation of putting the client into a situation where their free flow of discussion about their worries becomes pigeon holed. In other words, the counsellor should not say 'Yes, I can understand how worried you must be about your marriage but please will you tell me about the bullying that brought you here'.

It is also important, at this stage, that the counsellors understand that they do not need to seek fine detail and offer solutions. Their main activity is to view the range of concerns, each in its turn, and show interest and support, with little attempt at evaluation. This process can best be thought of one whereby the client and counsellor are together listing the concerns they want to debate and are trying to get together an agenda for further meetings.

This period of preparation can be vital for many clients and counsellors may well encounter a number of difficulties that make this period unhappily shorter or longer:

- The client is too emotional to be able to move rapidly from 'feelings' to problem description. Many clients need time to find the right words to describe their emotions and must get this out of the way before they can begin to think systematically. Some clients never move beyond this into a logical debate about resolution. Fortunately these are in the minority but even so, for many traumatised but otherwise sensible people it may take a few contact sessions before they are able to put their feelings aside long enough to debate strategies.

- The client is obsessed with one particular difficulty and fails to take account of its antecedents. This has to be handled very sensitively by the counsellor. On the one hand the client must not feel 'chopped off' but on the other, the counsellor does need to move on to other problems that may have more relevance. It is important that the client is reassured that there will be time later to return to that difficulty if the client wishes.

- The counsellor identifies a problem of which the client seems to be unaware. For an empowerment process which depends on a working partnership between counsellor and client there must be total honesty. Counsellors are free to voice their opinions provided that they do so in a way which does not imply that their opinions are of greater worth than the clients. Once identified the counsellors' perceptions of difficulties take no greater weight than those of the clients.

- The client will disclose only one problem and attempts to hide other relevant difficulties. This often happens in bully-victim situations. It may be that the victims really have done or continues to do something that draws the negative attentions of bullies to them. This does not justify bullying but nevertheless the counsellor must become aware of these antecedent behaviours so that they can be 'listed' for future discussions. It is undesirable and intrusive to delve for problems that the client is unwilling to impart but, on the other hand, the counsellor must make clear that there is less likelihood of success if vital information is left undiscussed.

Once the counsellor and the client have made their list of the difficulties they must then examine them in turn in more detail. The movement from simple scanning to detailed evaluation must be clearly signalled so that the client is aware that there is now a shift of emphasis. The counsellor now carefully and gently uncovers details about each of the difficulties listed, using open-ended questions to encourage specificity from the client. The questions are largely of the what, who, when, where, why, and how type (Priestley, McGuire, Flegg, Helmsley and Welham, 1978). Each problem is then thrashed out in such a way that its contribution to the overall difficulty of the client is established. Counsellors should not be putting words into the client's mouth during this phase, the questions are enough, the client should also refrain from trying to supply solutions. The trick is to listen carefully to ask detailed questions and to focus attention on the clients who, having experienced this approach, will feel valued, know their problems are being taken seriously and that they are being given time to find the right words to express whatever complexities need to be described.

This activity can encounter difficulties, some of which are now discussed.

- Too many concerns have been identified for adequate discussion of each. Both clients and counsellors can find it extremely tiring to investigate many problems in considerable detail; as a consequence it is generally better to draw up a 'short list' of no more than five. These can then be considered in detail.

• Some clients find it difficult to be specific in their answers. It is a fact that the vast majority of conversations we have are framed in terms of generalities. Most people are not used to an investigation that involves giving highly specific answers to questions. Particularly where the behaviours of bullying are concerned, many clients will not wish to give the specificity the counsellor requires, instead they have a need to dwell on the emotions surrounding the events rather than on the events themselves. They can feel perplexed and challenged by coun-sellors who insist on detail. The need for the detail has to be carefully explained and any persistent difficulty in giving details should be discussed together because the client may have some 'hidden agenda' which could influence the whole process of intervention.

• Identified problems frequently alter when details are given. Although it can be frustrating to the counsellor, it is generally a healthy matter when the clients discover that the problem they are describing in detail are not quite what they were in the first place. Often the act of being specific helps clients to reformulate their difficulties and so they come to see the problem in a new light.

• Keeping track of the details: most professional counsellors who practice task-centred approaches make notes. They often explain to the clients that they need to take notes because what the clients have to say is important and they (the counsellors) do not want to rely solely on their memory. The vast majority of clients accept note taking and it can help if the notes are readily visible to both client and counsellor. A flip chart is a good way of doing this so that both can agree what has been said and on the detail it contains.

• New topics are introduced at this stage. Although the preparatory process should have identified the list of problems to be discussed there is no embargo on bringing up new topics. If this happens once or twice then the counsellor should listen carefully and allow the new topics to take their place on the list. If, however, clients persists in bringing in new topics then it may be that they have few specific details to give about anything and that the problems are more imaginary than real. This does not mean that their problems should be discarded because a problem perceived by someone is a problem that person has, irrespective of how accurate their perceptions are. It does suggest, however, that a task-centred approach may not be realistic for such clients and what they need is a longer term opportunity to ventilate nonspecific emotions and gain support from so doing. Project staff are unlikely to be the best people for that purpose.

Prioritising the Problems: The next step, if possible, is to help the clients rank their listed problems and to choose which one or two, never more than three, shall be worked on. Although the choice is a matter of the clients' judgments in consultation with the counsellors, there is a worthwhile rule of thumb. This says that the best problems to prioritise are those that, if modified successfully, will also alleviate the others or some of the others. For example, in the context of bullying a client who lacks assertiveness may prioritise as her worst difficulty the harassment she receives in a particular shop. In her judgment, perhaps, that is the problem to be tackled and her judgment may be based upon seriously negative experiences whilst in that particular shop. Yet the counsellor will be aware that the real priority problem is her lack of assertiveness; if that were made good then she could assert herself in that shop and all other shops to prevent harassment.

In general terms considerations about problem priority are:

- Urgency

- Consequences

- The chances of success at reducing the problem

- The client's motivation to work on the problem

- The resources and support the client will need to work on the problem

- The ability of the counsellor and, possibly, the resources of the project to reduce the problem.

Finally, the specific nature of the problem will also have to be taken into account. In some cases of bullying the prioritised problem may have some features which mean that although it is important to the client it is not desirable to make significant changes. For example, where the client has identified bullying rising from racial prejudice it would not be wise to accede to demands to initiate positive discrimination wherever the bullying is taking place. Such a course of action would only deepen the problem.

The last comment indicates that this stage of prioritising problems may not always go smoothly between client and counsellor. One of the most common difficulties is that the client wishes to prioritise a problem which is not one that the counsellor would have selected. Under these circumstances the counsellor should generally go ahead and accept the client's judgment; after all this project is about empowerment and the creation of equal partnerships between clients and project workers so it is most unlikely that the counsellors would ever try to insist that their prioritised problem took precedence. This does not mean that counsellors should meekly accept the judgment of the clients and in the honest relationship that should exist the counsellors will have to be clear about their preferences and the reasons why.

Clients may agree to include the counsellors' problem priority as the second to be worked on during the intervention phase. One client of the writer was determined that the priority problem to be tackled was the apparent indifference of her daughter's headmaster in accepting that there was bullying in his school. The author, however, felt that the most important problem was the over-protectiveness of the client towards her daughter which was creating behaviour from the daughter that were the antecedent to her victimisation. After a long and frank discussion the client agreed that she would accept my concerns at a second level of priority provided that I agree to work with her on strategies for influencing the headteacher.

Stage Two — Setting Goals and Deadlines

Working through this stage requires clients to change the style of their thinking. The first stage was largely about what the problem is whereas this stage is about what is needed to put the problem right. This fundamental question of 'what is needed' is the only basis on which goals can be agreed. Many clients are afraid to make this transition because they know that they will be required to do something, they are aware that the counsellor is unwilling and unable to take the problem away from them so they recognise that the 'crunch' has come. Their anxiety arises because they may have attempted to do something in the past and failed; they do not want to fail again because they know that that could make their situation even worse. On the other hand they are aware that should they be successful their sense of accomplishment will be important to them because they are people who have experienced psychological pain as well as a lack of personal autonomy.

Often a restatement of the problem leads to a non-threatening goal. For example, if the client states the problem as 'My son always get bullied on Monday afternoons after P.E.', a restatement of that into its positive form 'on Monday afternoons my son will come home happily after P.E.' provides a goal that is unthreatening and yet infinitely desirable. The goal should be related to the problem but at times it may be indirect. Thus 'The biggest problem is that my daughter is terrified of walking home on her own when her friends stay for music practice' could be turned into a goal which says something like 'My daughter will join the aerobics club which finishes at the same time as music practice so that she can come home with her friends'. Careful statement of goals can lead to them being much less threatening; in accepting them the clients may experience a sense of relief and a feeling of self-confidence large enough to carry them through this rather difficult stage.

Most goals turn out to be statements of what clients want. A key factor in this stage is for the counsellor to be firmly aware of the need of the client that successfully achieving the goal will meet. It is important that the process is not rushed and that all options are considered before the final 'want' decision is made. It is seldom that the first and most obvious goal is the best. If clients understand that the 'want' they are working towards is the best possible solution for their predicament then they are likely to be more motivated than they would do towards a goal they had accepted reluctantly.

A second key factor for counsellor consideration is 'practicality'. It is all too easy for the counsellor and the client to be carried away on a wave of enthusiasm for a particular goal and to ignore the constraints that the client will encounter when trying to achieve that goal in his or her home area. For example, one client whose five year old son was being bullied found that she was becoming a victim as the little boy came home and took his unhappiness out on her. His temper tantrums with her were something to behold and she and the counsellor decided that ignoring them for longer and longer periods would be an appropriate strategy. What neither took into account as they discussed this goal was that the little family lived in a small terrace house with extremely thin walls. This made ignoring the loud screaming, crying and stamping an impossibility when two rather irate elderly people next door complained bitterly every time a pin dropped.

The counsellor, thereforere must always ask to what extent the client has the resources and the control necessary to obtain the goal. If the client has little control or few resources that relate to the goal then there is no likelihood of success. In addition, it is worth counsellors remembering that goals which involve changing other people's behaviour are much less likely to be attained than those which involve clients changing their own behaviour.

The third important factor for counsellors to consider is the 'desirability' of the goal. Some goals may seem highly desirable for the client but if they are attained may be undesirable for someone else, unless it is the bully whose power balance should be eroded. Empowering one person should never rest on a process that leads to the disempowerment of someone else. Where harm could come to a third party the counsellor would be wise to explain gently to the client why the project cannot be involved in helping the client move towards that goal.

The final step in this stage is to decide on a time limit. Logically this is set at a realistic point that both client and counsellor can agree . A highly specific goal which is totally within the client's control and resources will not take so long to achieve as one that the client must negotiate with other people and resources to obtain. It is also true that time limits should not be so short that failure is likely to occur and damage clients' motivation, yet on the other hand it is not desirable to allow clients to have too long to achieve their goals. Lengthy time limits encourage a 'I'll do it tomorrow' philosophy which often ends up with clients doing absolutely nothing. In addition long time limits are bad for the project. The briefer the period of counsellor involvement with clients the better in that more clients can be dealt with and the speedier the project itself will move towards its goals.

Related to the time limits is the schedule of counselling sessions. The author has discovered that many counsellors believe that sessions should always be weekly. There is nothing to substantiate that view; for some clients a rapid throughput of sessions with, perhaps two or three per week, may lead to a brief period of intervention before success. Other clients may have a fairly rapid one or two sessions during which their problems are explored and prioritised followed by fairly lengthy periods between sessions when they are engaged in working towards particular goals. The counsellor sees them merely to monitor their progress and to help them refine their strategies if necessary.

It is often a good idea to embody the frequency of sessions and a total number of sessions in a 'contract' which clearly lays out what is to be achieved by when for the client and what the counsellor must offer in order to help the client get there. Contracts can be very useful for clients who are happy to ventilate their feelings but less willing to consider solutions. In any event it is always desirable that the agreed goal and the time limit are written down with a copy for both client and counsellor. Copies may also be given to other people who are involved in the intervention such as class teachers in the case of child bullying. This written schedule should have the force of an agreement between counsellor and client to set the task-centred nature of the work firmly and to provide a reminder, particularly to the client, of what has been agreed and why. Infringement of this contract by the client could lead to loss of support by the project.

Stage Three: Setting the Task

Establishing the goals and the time limits during which they should be met is important and revealing. It leads naturally to the processes by which the goals are met, the 'how' stage. What is required now is the establishment of tasks, which are small steps taken towards meeting the goal. In many ways there are parallels to the concept of task analysis, heavily used in behavioural psychology to enable learning disabled people to move from a state of low skill in a particular area to a state of higher skill (McBrian and Foxen, 1981). The small steps are necessary because learning is best achieved and consolidated when people are given a comfortable progression of gentle movements rather than a huge leap forward to accomplish. So, in the case of task-centred intervention, the tasks are the segments of work to be done by the client, with the support of the counsellor, in order that the client moves steadily forward towards the goal. Some writers (e.g. Doel and Marsh, 1992) conceptualise tasks as the rungs of the ladder which start where the problem is as presented and reaches upwards to a better future; one where the problem has been resolved or at least alleviated. From this stage the tasks are considered during each counselling session. The sessions begin with an examination of the work that has already been done and then consider the next tasks along this metaphorical ladder.

Designing and Developing Tasks: Many of the factors which determine whether or not a goal is appropriate also apply to the design and development of tasks. Thus clients must find the task feasible so that the chances of success are high (failure is a corrosive force) and it should motivate the clients because they can clearly understand why, if the task is completed, it helps movement towards the goal.

It is important for clients to realise that tasks are not necessarily to be over and done with. Some tasks might be continuously rehearsed throughout the period of intervention; thus, for example, when a victim is learning to assert herself more effectively in the shops she goes to and outside the school gates where she picks up her children, then whatever strategies of assertion are given to her should be rehearsed consistently every time she finds herself in these settings. Some tasks of this sort are very often rehearsed in the counselling sessions. The client learning to assert herself may actually engage in brief role play sessions where the counsellor takes the part of a harassing neighbour or a bullying head-teacher and the client learns how to respond effectively in the security of the counselling session The client may also discover that the tasks are reciprocated, that is they are on a 'I'll do this if you do that' basis. For example one client was required to escort her eight year old son to within 50 yards of the school gates as a means of preventing the bullying that usually occurred soon after he left his home alone. Up until that time the client had preferred to remain in the house watching early morning television than take up this escort duty. It made made clear that if she wished to have further support from the project (not the counselling sessions) she would need to enter into a contract stating that continuing support was dependent upon her escort task.

A great deal of creativity and imagination is necessary in establishing tasks. Although the counsellor may see what kinds of tasks are appropriate in moving up the rungs of the ladder it is helpful if the clients themselves supply the 'find tuning' to tasks which make them practical within the resources they have available. For example, in another situation where a parent was going to provide more support to her child bullied on the way home from school by escorting him, the counsellor was pleased to hear her put forward the possibility that this escorting should be done dis-creetly rather than overtly. The client felt that her son would be 'rubbished' further in the eyes of his peers if, at the age of nearly 10 years he was seen to be taken home from school by his mother. She felt that she could supervise him just as well if she went to the Post Office at that time every day to post off the orders from her mail order catalogue job. This would give her a reason for being out of the house and near the school that ostensibly had little to do with protecting her child. This is an example of a client thinking creatively to facilitate the task.

Reviewing Tasks: Each session in this third stage begins with an appraisal of how the tasks previously set have been completed, and with what success. Lots of positive reinforcement should be given for successes and failures should be reframed as opportunities for modifying the tasks by breaking them down to yet further steps in order that the client can be successful in the future. It is important that the client does not perceive any kind of disappointment or blame from the counsellor and it is important also that the counsellor does not merely brush aside failure in a jovial attempt at being encouraging by making comments like 'Oh well! Better luck next time' — the message this gives to the client is that the task wasn't terribly important in the first place.

This review process can throw up a number of difficulties; here are some of the most common:

- The client gets diverted by other events and movement towards the goal loses its direction: Where the problems have persisted for a long time it is quite likely the clients get into bad habits of responding for them. To the observer these bad habits may seem to be illogical and chaotic yet, to some extent they have served the clients because they represent a form of coping. Task-centred approached are very powerful but it is hard to break into established faulty response styles and care should be taken to provide the clients with an understanding of early signals that they should respond to before their habitual patterns take over. In one case, for example, the client was a 30 year old woman in need of more assertiveness; she agreed that one task she should complete and continuously rehearse was to stay on the same side of the street as a particularly harassing neighbour who the client lived in fear of. There was no history of verbal of physical assault on the client by this neighbour but the neighbour had a reputation for both forms of intimidation and the client sensed from the woman's expression her aggressive intent whenever the client got close to her. Rather than let this happen the client would walk to the other side of the road and carry on to the shops. The client agreed that this got over the immediate problem but was making her feel small and stupid each time it happened. Therefore the task of remaining on the same side of the street was appropriate. On review, however, the counsellor found that on no occasion in the intervening two weeks between sessions had the client been able to accomplish this task. On deeper investigation the counsellor discovered that the client had got into an almost unconscious habit of looking out of her own front door and judging whether the harassing neighbour was around or not. If the neighbour's front door was closed and the curtains drawn then the client realised that the woman was probably out somewhere and felt safe to leave her own home and go to the shops. These details had not come to light during the problem scanning stage and so had not been taken account of. The review therefore revealed that the task was not feasible because the client was never allowing herself to be in a position where it was. The obvious adjustments were made and a new task formulated.

- The client loses motivation: Sometimes when the review establishes that the task or tasks have not been completed, the reasons given by the clients may seem vague, non-specific or deliberately evasive. This happens when the client has 'run out of steam', there is no motivation to accomplish the task. The counsellor then needs to establish whether this lack of motivation is specific to the task that has not been accomplished, a general lack of motivation for the whole intervention or is indicative that the problem no longer exists or has lost its severity for the client.

- The client says that not only the task is completed but the goal is completed: it is rare that a really rapid movement towards the goal can be achieved on the basis of only one or two completed tasks. If this is the case then it is quite likely that the goal was too simple or even inappropriate. Rather than this be a cause for celebration, it should be a stimulus for reviewing the goal set in the first place. In general terms goals require several tasks to be completed satisfactorily before they can said to have been attained.

Finishing a Task-Centred Intervention

The intervention should cease as soon as the problem specified in the written agreement drawn up at the beginning has been accomplished. This does not necessarily mean a loss of all contact between client and counsellor but it implies that a particular phase has been completed.

The actual ending is marked by a period of evaluation. Has the client genuinely achieved what was required? Now that the process has been worked through, were the goals selected the right ones in the first place? If the client announces satisfaction then the counsellor must emphasise what the client has done to achieve success because this continues the process of empowerment.

The clients' views on the process should also be sought. This is not just a matter of quality control, which is an important ambition in its own right, it is also an opportunity to emphasise the sequences the clients have come through. The clients can then be encouraged to use those sequences again in the future if the same or similar problems arise. Unfortunately, however, the endings of interventions will not always be smoothly brought about, there are common difficulties:

- The goal is not achieved successfully: if all that is needed is some extra time then there is no harm in extending the limit. But if the client seems to be incapable of ever meeting the goal then extending the limit merely gives that person more opportunity for failure. It may be that the client does not favour the task-centred approach but really wants something of a more psychotherapeutic nature in order to examine feelings, negative emotions and talk through the problems rather than try to tackle them. It would be unusual if this kind of difficulty was not apparent at some point earlier on in the intervention in which case it is better to terminate it than to end up in the situation whereby client and counsellor are almost looking for someone to blame.

- The client does not want the relationship with the counsellor to finish: it is quite common for clients to become very dependent on counsellors. Most can accept that there will be an end to the counselling relationship and whilst they may not look forward to it they can nevertheless work towards it. Some clients, however, will wish to sidetrack the task-centred approach into one that will take longer but will provide them with the supportive company they associate with the counsellor. This difficulty should not be regarded as a weakness on the part of the client as many victims of bullying are fairly lonely people within their communities and the opportunity to talk to someone who is sympathetic and helpful does not come often to them. Where loneliness or isolation is a factor then the project, if not the counsellor, has a responsibility to pass the client to another situation which can be supportive. A good one arises when the client also provide a service to victims. For this reason counsellors should be made aware of other voluntary agencies in the community that are engaged in support work and encourage clients who find difficulty in terminating the relationship because of loneliness to meet up with people in these groups.

The Task-Centred Approach: some final words

This approach is not mutually exclusive. The fact that the project tends to use it in the context of counselling victims does not mean that it cannot also offer other forms of support and intervention. There is no reason that there should not be a prolonged period of occasional monitoring and support for all victims who have worked through it but who periodically need contact with the project to 'refresh' themselves. Counsellors who do not find themselves in sympathy with the task centred approach may wish to engage in this less intensive but longer lasting form of support. It is important, however, that the long term support work does not overtake or supplant the task-centred approach in terms of its relative importance to the project. Project workers will find that there are many more victims then they can cope with and there will be a need to work through quickly, efficiently and skilfully with this group of oppressed people. The fact that it is a partnership which takes account of the creativity, opinions and resources of the client makes it attractive to many of the mainstream of today. There is a current move now amongst user-groups to resist approaches whereby the worker implies that they know best and the client should follow advice. Such an attitude defies and ultimately defeats empowerment and the kind of project that this book describes cannot survive in the face of it.

The Orientation of the Counselling Service in the context of the Community Project

From what has gone before it is clear that the counselling of victims is largely based on a short-term task-centred approach with the aim of improving client assertiveness using strategies which fit within the empowerment model underpinning the whole project. Counselling from such a perspective must therefore be orientated towards:-

- Assisting clients to develop and improve options for changing their behaviour as victims;

- Helping clients to understand the consequences of particular behaviours, including their own submissive or placatory behaviours where these exist;

- Improving clients' accessing of personal and social resources available to them either directly or indirectly through their family and social networks;

- Reinforce the development of clients' belief in their personal potency and efficacy as fully functioning members of the community, and

- encourage client perceptions of having competences rather than deficits.

Supervision of the Counsellors

The orientation given above is a tall order for counsellors, no matter how good their training might be. What they should know and be trained to utilise is covered elsehere (Randall, 1995) but, on the assumption that individual counsellors have gone through an approved training process satisfactorily, it is still necessary to supervise their work on a regular and sometimes irregular basis to ensure that what they are offering the clients is of the highest possible quality and does no harm. This should not be set up in such a way that counsellors will feel that Big Brother is watching them. Indeed they should be encouraged to regard themselves as independent counsellors but whose practice is accountable to the project. There are three essential strands to establishing this accountability in personal development.

1. Personal Supervision: The counselling service offered by a community anti-bullying project must be committed to the maximum development of the counsellors working within it. The best policy is to ensure that the counsellors understand they are functioning independently but within a code of practice that allows for accountability.

2. Supervision: Each counsellor should be assigned to a personal supervisor at the completion of the training and for a probationary period. At this time a brief skills review of performance should be provided by a Counselling Services Supervisor and that review should be the basis for an initial supervision contract. Each counsellor should meet with his or her supervisor for at least one hour each month during which time professional development goals are reviewed, extended and strategies put in place for improvement. Ideally this process should finish with a performance review at the end of the probationary period which may well signal a good time to hand the counsellor on to another supervisor. It is not generally a good idea for counsellors to retain the same supervisor for long periods, both can fall into a rut of complacency and, in addition, the provision of new supervisors may well lead to fresh ideas for the development of counsellors.

Implementation of development goals should be managed through an ongoing monitoring and feedback system provided by the Counselling Services Manager. There should be regular opportunities for the discussion of progress, preferably at weekly review meetings, which involve both the Counselling Services Manager and the personal supervisors of the counsellors.

3. Performance Review: The performance review process should begin at the start of the probationary phase of each counsellor's training and ideally is continued as a six monthly process leading up to the supervisory hand over. This process creates a environment in which the counsellors, the Counselling Service Manager and, ultimately, the Implementation Group may clearly understand the expectations each has of the other. The review process is completed by the personal supervisors and should be fully discussed with the counsellors as part of the hand over process which must logically involve both the outgoing and incoming supervisors, the Counselling Services Manager and each counsellor.

The main theme of the review is feedback on performance during the period and to provide professional development goals for a further six month period. These goals must then be developed through personal supervision. At the completion of the review each counsellor must make written comments on the content of the review to complete the document which then becomes part of the counsellors' professional development record.

Monitoring

The counselling services should be supervised by at least one Counselling Service Manager who should be part of the Implementation Group. If the project offers 24 hour counselling, which is an expensive but useful luxury, then there may well be two counselling services managers to reflect a shift system. One major task of the Counselling Services Manager is to monitor performance, provide support to counsellors and also offer a debriefing service.

Debriefing is the provision of 'counselling for the counsellors' and can be vital whenever a counsellor becomes excessively stressed or overly involved in the counselling of their clients. A further responsibility of the Counselling Services Manager is to establish appropriate ongoing monitoring of individual counsellor performance which helps the identification of individual training and/or support needs. These can then be built in to the ongoing professional development plans.

Promoting the Concept and Practice of Supervision

There is no doubt that accountability at every level is a daunting prospect for many people, professionals as well as volunteers. Many feel that it is an intrusion upon them and a possible reflection on their level of skill. All volunteer counsellors must, therefore, understand the necessity for the supervision arrangements. They must realise that the ultimate effectiveness of the counselling service relies to a considerable extent on the quality of the counsellors and, in turn, the quality of the counsellors depends very significantly on training and professional development opportunities which are available to them. Failure to establish a high quality of service will lead to a thwarting of the clients' needs at a time when they contact the service. This may have very serious ramifications for the clients: after all if one buys a stale loaf of bread it can be simply taken back to the shop, if one attempts to engage in counselling with a poor counsellor then the problem becomes greater and there is no where to take it back to.

THE HOTLINE AND TELECOUNSELLING SERVICE

The developing trends in community mental health services during the 1960s and 70s saw a variety of new approaches to intervention unfolding. Of these the advent of telephone counselling was probably most dramatic. Telephone hotline and crisis services sprang up throughout the western world such that within five years the word 'hotline' became familiar to just about everybody. By 1973 there were over 500 crisis telephone services in the United States alone (Stein and Lambert, 1984) but no-one appears to know how many there are throughout the world today. They are obviously an important community resource and one that the Implementation Group cannot ignore as a means of getting help to victims and of reaching a wide audience within the targeted community.

Both philosophical and pragmatic arguments have been given to support the utilisation of telephone counselling and referral services. An important reason is that telephone counselling systems appear to serve a very broad cross-section of the community and so will reach groups of people who might not otherwise have tried to access more traditional counselling services (Iscoe, Hill, Harmon and Coffman, 1979). So amongst young people, hotlines appear to be used frequently by dis-affected adolescents who are dissatisfied with traditional sources of help, such as parents and teachers (Aspler and Hoople, 1976). Some inter-vention system work is aimed at the specific needs of minority groups, (eg. Enright and Parsons, 1976). Secondly, the ease of being able to make contact anonymously is attractive to many hotline users (McCord and Packwood, 1973). Indeed many clients have told me that not only does the telephone counselling service appeal to them but also that the answer-phone service attached to it outside normal working hours is also an affective release for them when they have felt particularly scared or upset: the sound of the counsellors' answering message is a support in its own right.

Perhaps more importantly, since the telephone is an integral part of nearly everybody's life it can provide an immediate intervention without the stress of plucking up courage to make a self-referral and then having to wait several weeks or even months to get an appointment. Ease of availability is related to the matter of cost; even when face-to-face coun-selling services are freely available many clients are unable or unwilling to spend the money in travelling to the counselling centre. Best of all, according to many of my clients, they always feel in control; as one said 'If I don't like what I'm hearing or saying, I just put the phone down'.

As the telephone allows direct access to support for a wide range of callers who may not otherwise have sought help on a face-to-face basis it therefore maximises the opportunities for short-term intervention for many clients, including those who have clearly identified difficulties, those who are not certain whether they want help but want to test out the service and those who simply want someone to wave a magic wand and come up with an instant cure.

Telephone counselling is now utilised by a bewildering variety of crisis response services and increasingly has become an important diagnostic and preventative tool in health education. A characteristic of many telephone counselling services is their orientation towards problems solving in as few a number of contacts as possible. This sits well with the Task-Centred approach.

In a community anti-bullying project this orientation suits both the needs of bullied clients and the need to protect scarce project resources. Accordingly a particular style of task-centred intervention is recommended to the Implementation Group; that is the form of intervention known as Solution-focussed Counselling. This is primarily attributable to the work of de Shazer who has written extensively on the subject of brief therapy (de Shazer, 1985, 1991). His solution-focussed approach offers well-documented and efficient brief therapy techniques, most of which transfer effectively to the medium of the telephone.

The approach is based on a clear sequence of steps which guide the first interview. The first simply asks the client to give details of the problem and to clarify these as far as it is possible. Next the client is asked to give 'exceptions' to the problems that are described. In this context exceptions refers to occasions that the problem does not arise despite the probability that it will. For example, one client made the comment that 'She always gets the better of me in the office. I never seem to be able to assert myself'. When asked, 'Do you mean that every single time that you see this woman she gets you to do or say something that you don't want to?'. The client then replied 'Well, no, not every time'. These exceptions are then explored to determine what it is about the exceptional circumstances that have stopped the client's own rule from becoming reality yet again. These exceptions then form the basis of an intervention which tries to make exception the rule for the client. In the case of the woman just mentioned she was able to discover how on the exceptional occasions she was able to assert herself against the woman who had been bullying her and practice this much more frequently.

Goals then have to be clarified, this is sometimes best carried out by scaling the answers to questions. For example, on a scale of 0-10, (10 meaning that a client has total control over the problem, and 0 meaning that the client has no control), it is possible to get the clients to determine where they are now. Then, once they have provided a figure to go on this scale they are asked 'Where do you want to be?' The scale allows the client a loose kind of target to aim at, the figure representing a state of feeling good or not depending on how far up or down the scale it is. Sometimes attached to the use of this scale is something called a 'miracle' question; this is a variation of 'If you woke up tomorrow and a miracle had happened, how would things be? What would be better? What important thing would have changed in your life?' This also assists in clarification of goals and can be helpful when formulating a solution to the problem.

de Shazer introduces into his face-to-face consultations a break or pause in the process. Client and counsellor leave each other for 10-15 minutes and de Shazer (1985) believes that this is important because it helps the client to rebuild response attentiveness, which is the ability to focus on precise problematic issues and their solutions. This break is even more easily managed in the medium of telephone counselling in that the caller can be asked to call back again after several hours or, in some cases, the next day. This not only gives clients an opportunity to reappraise their problems but also gives counsellors opportunity to discuss possible solutions with co-workers. Where no co-workers are present the counsellors still have an opportunity to reflect on what clients have told them and begin to fashion strategies for solutions.

At the time of the return call the counsellors delivers a message to their clients. This message is made up of several common features. These include compliments, comments about the problem, reframing the problem and, possibly, a task. Given that the counselling service set up by the Implementation Group has a task-centred focus this latter part of the message is particularly important.

How the message is delivered depends very much on the nature of the client at the other end of the phone. de Shazer (1985) speaks of three types of client in the context of face-to-face counselling. The first type is the 'visitor', a caller with no real reason to be in the counselling situation, a person who is not really interested in solving the problem. Conversely a 'customer' is a client who really wants to do something about the problem and is keen to seek help. The third type, the 'complainant', has a complaint about other people but also some expectation that things can be improved. The telephone counsellors' job is to decide which of these three types any particular caller is and then to modify the message accordingly. Clearly customers can be moved fairly swiftly from reframing the problem into solutions that explore exceptions. The complainants, on the other hand may well have strong feelings to ventilate before they can go forward to exploring the ways in which exceptions can lead to strategies. Visitors will quickly be put off by a rapid move into problem solving with them as the responsible person. It is invariably the case that such clients are not suited to telephone counselling but are likely, if the problem worsened, to seek face-to-face counselling at a later date.

It may be seen from these brief comments that the solution-focussed approach can be extremely effective when clients can be dealt with through the medium of telephone counselling alone. In embarking on such an approach the Implementation Group must ensure that their telephone counsellors recognise the benefits of telephone counselling and do not simply regard the telephone as a means of making appointments for face-to-face sessions. Instead they must see it as a powerful community strategy assisting in the support of victims who might otherwise be too scared to seek help.

CHAPTER 9

Putting the strategies in place

By now everything should be in place — all resources identified, strategy plans drawn up and staff and volunteers trained. The media has carried introductory stories; various institutions such as shops and pubs are alerted and pamphlets and posters are placed everywhere. The counsellors are ready for the first victims and the hotline is waiting to ring.

This is a massive accomplishment of the Steering and Implementation Groups but it will all be wasted if there are no strategies to support the structures. This chapter presents an overview of suitable strategies. It does not describe them in depth because they are already well recorded elsewhere and the sources of this information are given. Sufficient detail is provided, however, for the Implementation Group to decide which strategies to prioritise, research and put in place.

The strategies are presented in three distinct groups. The first is the Schools Group; a set of strategies that will support within-school anti-bullying policy once the bully audit has been completed. All the strategies are well-tried and researched, given time they will reduce within-school bullying if used consistently and with commitment. The second group is the Link Group, a set of strategies which build upon the work done in the schools to involve parents, families and the broader community. Positive involvement of school staff and people from the community served by the schools provide the essential link between the proactive and preventative work of the project and its therapeutic intervention with those already bullied and oppressed.

The third group, the Community Group, is a set of strategies that will support the work done within the community to raise awareness of bullying and mobilise people against it.

Group 1: The School Group

Those members of the project who will work most closely with the schools and carry into them the training required to implement the strategies listed below should read in depth a number of books which deal with school bullying. Of these three stand out as being of particular worth in the context of strategies:

> Tattum, D.P. and Lane, D.A. (eds) (1989), Bullying in Schools; Stoke-on-Trent, Trentham.

> Tattum, D.P. and Graham (1993), Countering Bullying: Initiatives by School and Local Authorities, Stoke on Trent: Trentham.

Also, the 'practice manual' from an in depth research study on the subject of bullying:

> Sharpe, S. and Smith, P.K. (1994), Tackling Bullying in Your School, London: Routledge.

Although other books and resources are listed in this chapter (Appendix A) these three will provide most of the material necessary to engage with school staff beyond the awareness raising level.

The strategies that follow within the Schools Group are subdivided into three sub-groups which, from the writer's experience, represent the best progression through strategies. These sub-groups are:

- Curriculum issues

- Responding to Bullying

- Prevention of Bullying

1. Curriculum Issues

Of the three sub groups, the first examines how schools can make a curriculum issue of bullying thereby bringing it to the attention of all children as part of their personal and social development. This is a vital process because it is not sufficient simply to teach pupils that bullying is against the school rules; they most also learn why it is wrong and, more particularly, why they should not be simple bystanders watching the victimisation of others. Making an anti-bullying theme part of this personal/social curriculum will help to create a positive school environ-ment in which bullying cannot thrive because the pupils will have the social understanding to monitor and report it rather than to treat it as somebody else's business. In so doing children are far less likely to sup-port bullies by witnessing their deeds and appearing to approve of them. This means that a substantial social reinforcer for school-based bullying will no longer exist for those pupils for whom bullying is a means of obtaining social approval.

This strategy of making bullying a curriculum issue is a vital first step towards the establishment of a whole-school policy against bullying. In the longer term if all the schools throughout the community practice the same curriculum theme then it is more likely that the children's awareness will pervade the community through their parents.

Sharpe and Smith (1994) state that raising awareness of bullying behaviour and of the schools anti-bullying policy will require between two and three hours of curriculum time each year. However, they state that to maintain awareness, challenge and change the behaviour of bullying and the attitudes that children hold require a more prolonged and intensive effort (page 42). They write that teachers will need to repeat the anti-bullying theme regularly during the school year by making it a part of lessons and assemblies and identify a number of strategies for doing this.

Role-Play and Drama: Many children and adults find it almost impossible to tackle difficult and painful issues because the feelings evoked are too painful for them to bear and they retreat. Experience of counselling distressed employees subject to severe personal harassment at work show that these feelings are often so powerful that the employees have sought redeployment or resigned rather than utilise perfectly satis-actory personal harassment procedures. Bullying and harassment are therefore amongst the many issues that some children and as many adults will retreat from.

Drama can help such children tackle the issues without evoking the feelings at an unbearable level of severity. There is a distancing effect that role-play or drama can produce which makes the issue bearable. Often this can be made more overt for the child victim by placing the character of the victim in another child of a similar age but opposite gender. As the re-sources section shows drama has been used by professionals in the form of standard productions to tackle successfully various aspects of bullying including the issue of racist bullying. The use of such plays can be a powerful weapon in the schools' armoury against bullying but it is im-portant for staff to realise that they should not merely use role-play or drama to tackle bullying alone. It is important that other important aspects of the personal/social curriculum also receive their representation through this medium.

Whenever role play or drama is used to impart a social message to pupils, it is most successfully used as the precursor to small group or class discussion about the various facts, issues, attitudes and feelings which are invoked dramatically. In the context of bullying such dramatic representations can examine a number of issues such as what makes a bully, the common family circumstance of bullies, who is most likely to become a victim, what motivates pupils to become bullies, what does bullying do to victims and their families and how it can be stopped.

In addition representation should weigh heavily on the bystander issue, namely that bystanders who fail to support victims are actually encouraging the bully and making the problem worse. The role of children who report bullying can be presented in a very proactive way and so help to diminish the commonly held attitude that to tell on bullies is a form of 'sneaking' or 'spragging'. Finally the role-play and drama strategies can be used to powerfully depict the personal experiences of victims in a manner which the majority of pupils can access and understand. The majority of victims do not tell anyone of their experiences and therefore it is quite likely that the majority of children who are neither bullies nor victims will have no real understanding of the true harm that bullying can do.

Curry and Sharpe (in Sharpe and Smith, 1994) present some detailed information on the use of role-play and drama to place bullying successfully within the personal/social curriculum. Their notes of guidance (pages 59-69) give ample information on how this powerful media can be used satisfactorily. They show how drama may be used to explore a number of important themes about bullying. One is the theme about the families that many bullies come from. Information given previously (Chapter 2) shows that many bullies do not come from happy, normally functioning families. Their parents may be cold, distant or demanding and aggressive. In many cases, the bullies themselves may be bullied by their own parents who use physically coercive styles of discipline. The role-play or drama established to teach this must depict the bullies as coming from a situation which is inferior to those of their victims. The object is not to secure strong and sympathetic support for bullies which may vindicate what they do but rather point out that some bully because their home lives are inadequate. They are not people to be admired, rather they are to be pitied. Such a representation diminishes a high status that bullies can enjoy amongst the 'bystander' group.

Schools in the targeted community should bring together their best pupil actors and actresses to stage a joint play for members of the community about bullying. The content of this play should accurately reflect the origins and the consequences of bullying as children experience them. The parenting dysfunctions, inappropriate reinforcement of the aggression and long term effects on both victims and bullies should be drawn out and placed within environmental contexts that are familiar to the audience. These would include a representation of the times and places where bullying is known to occur frequently; such 'landmarks' will help to place the anti-bullying theme within a familiar context.

Using Suitable Literature: Over the past decade much superb literature has been produced about bullying. The resources section at the end of this chapter presents some of these and they can be used to stimulate group discussion.

The Pupils' Own Bully-Audit: After the topic of bullying has been introduced through the use of role-play, drama and selected literature it is desirable if the pupils are involved in conducting a survey around the targeted community's schools and their localities to determine the frequency and type of bullying. Not only is this a valuable exercise leading to a further quantification of the problem but also it gives pupils, who are neither bullies nor victims, the opportunity to learn first-hand what bullying means to some children and how they suffer from it. As part of their report on the frequency and nature of bullying, pupils may also provide, suitably anonymised, first-hand personal accounts from victims.

2. Responding to Bullying

No matter how good a school's preventative measures may be, or how successfully anti-bullying attitudes are established through the personal/social curriculum, there will always be some incidence of bullying which is sufficiently severe to warrant particular strategies of intervention. This section is about the strategies that have been found useful.

One of the most effective strategies against bullying is simply to take notice of it and show the bullies how disgusting they are. Name-calling and teasing frequently respond to this because the bullies experience similar blows to their morale and self-esteem as do victims.

Any bully who persistently ignores sanctions and seems incapable of giving up aggression despite intervention, is in need of psychological treatment. Such pupils need help from educational psychology services provided by LEAs. The project team need to be in close contact with the providers of this service.

The project team needs to ensure that teachers and other influential people working in schools follow some 'golden rules' about dealing with incidents of bullying. These are:

- bullying causes immediate pain; deal with both bully and victim immediately the incident comes to light; record the incident, detailing what happened, who did what to whom and how the matter has been dealt with; do not bully the bullies, that provides them with a further model of adult aggression;

- immediate discussions with the bullies should be firm, fair and not allowed to fall into a lengthy diatribe. Bullying is always wrong and this point must be made clear and if necessary, supported by further disciplinary action;

- inform the parents of bullies and victims;

- resist staff members who argue that to acknowledge bullying in the school will weaken the schools' reputation in the community. What does weaken its reputation in the community is if teachers deny something that is no secret. Such schools lose respect in comparison with those who are honest and overtly problem-solving;

- if the bullying is occurring outside of school and close to community services such as shops then make contact with the shop owners/ managers and encourage them to report anything they witness in the vicinity to the school; where possible bring together pupils to discuss the problems of bullying and help them to reach possible solutions.

The No Blame Approach: This is a successful strategy for tackling bullying (Maines and Robinson, 1992) and has been derived from the influential work of the Swedish psychologist Anatol Pikas, working with the Education Department at Upsala University (1989). Although these methods have in common a concentration on finding a solution by sharing concern about it between teachers, victims and pupils, there are sufficient differences for them to merit separate inclusion in the strategies list.

• The 'No Blame Approach' is now used extensively throughout UK schools and there have been claims of a 95% success rate. There are a number of steps in this approach, usually seven, which teachers work through. During the first of these the victim is interviewed about who was involved and how he or she feels when being bullied. Descriptions can be supported by writing or drawing. The remaining steps require teaching staff to meet with all the people involved including bystanders and colluders, explaining the problem, ensuring that responsibility is shared between victims, bullies and colluders and then encouraging all those involved, except the victim, to provide ideas for solutions. In general the size of this decision making group should not exceed around eight and the teaching staff involved make clear that responsibility for solving the problem is left with them. Finally, usually about a week after this discussion, a teacher meets with each member of the group individually and discusses what progress has been made.

A main strength of this approach is that is makes bullies less likely to seek retribution from victims for informing on them but this is not always the case in practice. One of the main themes of Robinson and Maines is that resolution cannot be framed in terms of retribution; their aim does not concern justice or morality, but to change behaviour and so achieve a good outcome for victims. Not surprisingly, this theme has its critics.

The Method of Common Concern: This method is an essentially counselling-based approach for resolving group bullying situations. Anatol Pikas (1989) claims that it is particularly appropriate where one or more pupils are 'mobbed' on a regular basis by a group. The conventional wisdom is that it is only really suitable for pupils who are aged nine years old and upwards but the author is aware of some schools that have used it with modifications for much younger children and claimed success. The heart of this approach is an overt desire to establish rules that enable all pupils to work and live in the same school without aggressive behaviour. Wisely, it does not seek to make everyone friendly with everyone else and neither does it pretend to get at the truth underpinning all bullying situations — this is completely unrealistic when so much bullying is brought into schools as a consequence of inter-family aggression.

This method is described carefully and in great detail by Sharpe, Cowie and Smith (1994) and consists of three main stages:

- A teacher (or it could be a counsellor, psychologist, etc) has individual talks with each member of the mobbing group. These talks last approximately ten minutes and the teacher follows a prepared script.

- The same person talks to the victim of the mobbing and again follows a prepared script.

- About a week later the talks are repeated on an individual basis. The purpose of these meetings is to determine how well each pupil has managed to progress in relation to aims set during the previous meetings.

• A group meeting is then held following a particular format designed to evoke empathy from the mobbers. To begin with the teacher meets with the bullying group only, the victim is not included at this stage. The mobbers are then asked to make positive statements about the victim. These are used to gauge the degree of empathy that now exists. The victim is then asked to join the group to hear these statements repeated.

The following case example shows clearly how this approach has been used on one occasion:

Sally was a ten year-old plump girl with a bad complexion, poor state of hygiene and a thin rather whining voice. She was irritating to other girls in her class and was frequently complained about.

Apparently she had a habit of making unfortunate remarks about boys that some of the girls were becoming interested in. As a rather 'late developer' Sally didn't understand what the motivations were and made embarrassing remarks. Although probably not intended to offend some of these remarks were insensitive.

Her mother had an interview with the Headteacher and complained that Sally did not want to come to school, she was always having stomach aches and said she was being bullied. Sally had told her mother that a gang of girls were pushing her around, spitting on her, teasing her about her spots, telling her she had B.O. and scattering her belongings.

The school was currently in the process of implementing an anti-bullying policy and the Method of Common Concern was under evaluation. The Headteacher felt that it was appropriate in this case and asked the school's educational psychologist to use it with Sally.

The psychologist used a scripted interview with each member of the mobbing group. This started with the statement 'I hear that you have been very nasty to Sally'. The prevarications and excuses that followed this statement were ignored and followed with 'Why have these nasty things been done to Sally? Tell me about it'. Explanations followed which included accurate statements about Sally's provocative behaviour. These were noted and the most commonly occurring were highlighted for future change.

The final part of these initial interviews revolved around the question 'How can you help Sally now?' If the 'mobbers' made comments about what Sally should do, the psychologist interrupted and said firmly 'No, I asked what you could do to help Sally'. Comments like 'stop throwing her stuff around' were immediately reinforced ('That's a very good idea') and followed by an instruction to meet again in one week to see how the suggestion had worked out in practice.

The psychologist next interviewed Sally and again used a scripted set of questions. She was asked 'How often are these nasty things done to you?' to which the response was 'nearly every day'. She was asked 'How does it all start — what were you doing?' The information given was then checked out against the highlighted responses about Sally from the individual bullies.

Sally was asked what she might do to change her own provocative behaviour and, on saying that she would stop making rude remarks, the interview was terminated with verbal reinforcement and the comment 'We'll see how that works next week and meet again to discuss it'.

Finally, a group meeting was called of the bullies at the end of the week. Each was asked to say something positive about Sally who was later called in to hear these comments repeated. Amongst them were 'Sally would look really pretty if she washed her hair more', and 'Sally can be very kind when she's not making rude remarks' Subsequent interviews with Sally and her mother dealt with these issues sensitively.

Assertiveness Training:

Jimmy was an eleven year-old pupil of a large primary school in a deprived inner-city area. He had moved from a small isolated village because of the break-up of his parents' marriage.

From the first day Jimmy was subjected to taunts and teasing. Gradually the bullying took on a more physical form as a group of boys in his class began to push him, poke him from behind and punch him as they ran past laughing. None of them would individually pick a fight with him because he was a well-made boy and strong from farm work. When he confronted them they giggled and said it was only a game.

Eventually Jimmy attacked one of them in the playground and the teacher on duty did not believe that he had been teased. As a result only he got into trouble. The bullies seemed to feel that their actions were vindicated. Jimmy responded by spasmodic truancy and further attacks on his tormentors. He became a bully himself.

Two of the boys were badly bruised and and their parents complained. He was referred to an educational psychologist and child guidance teacher who reported that Jimmy lacked adequate social skills. His manner and social behaviour drew attention to him and although he could eventually stop others from picking on him, he could only do so through aggression.

Jimmy agreed with these comments and explained that he didn't know much about people because he had never known many. He hated life in the city because '... the people are loud, swear too much and they hurt you by saying nasty things'. He told the teacher 'I don't know how to stop them hurting me without hurting them worse'.

It was recommended that Jimmy attend a social skills group at the Child Guidance Centre where he could learn to assert himself without being aggressive. He learned how to keep calm and say' Don't do that: I don't like it', 'Do you enjoy being mean?', and 'Why do you like being cruel?' Although these comments were often ridiculed, the bullies did so with embarrassment and eventually left him alone.

Assertiveness Training has become part of the problem resolution of a number of different groups of clients including bullied children and adults. It is also found in negotiating strategies and work on decision making, 'people' management and conflict resolution. Although such training is usually given to groups it can be used with individual students who have difficulties in developing sufficient self-esteem to withstand the kinds of conflict situations which give rise to bullying such as name-calling.

It is not suitable for children of less than seven years of age who need adult protection from bullies. From seven onwards however it is a reasonable expectation that children who are well supported in their home environments will develop strategies from which self-esteem develops, that enable them to take an equal place within their peer group. Where children fail to develop such strategies and are seen by their teachers to have low self-esteem then assertiveness training is desirable.

There is, however, one caveat to go alongside these statements. It has already been noted that good levels of self-esteem do depend significantly on the support, stimulation and encouragement that the home provides. A child whose self-esteem is low may come from a home background that is inadequately supportive and, as a result, assertiveness training should only take place in parallel with discussions with parents. It is important that parents understand that this training is considered to be necessary for their child and that they engage fully in supporting it.

Parents often mistake assertion for aggression. They must understand that assertiveness training is the practice element of a philosophy of human rights that each individual has a unique contribution to make to society and an equal place within it from which the contribution can be made. The techniques themselves are generally geared to the particular life circumstances of the individual undertaking the training and are designed to present a mental 'set' of 'what to do when' strategies. Common experiences of assertiveness training are that such techniques provide people of all ages with a mental 'shield' which deflects the initial behaviour of bullies (usually verbal) and prevents it from escalating into something worse. After assertiveness training the trainees generally feel more control and are empowered to resist the bullies; their sense of bitterness, anger and despair gives way to one of confidence and 'These kids won't get the better of me'.

The key understanding for parents is that their children will in future stand up for their rights without harming those of other children. Their children will make assertive responses of verbal messages, direct eye contact and more assured body language, that communicates to potential bullies that they have no right to persist with their behaviour and that trouble will arise if they do.

One of the best programmes of assertiveness training is described by Sharpe, Cowie and Smith (1994) and aims to teach pupils how to:

- Make assertive statements

- Resist manipulation and threats

- Respond appropriately to name-calling

- Remove themselves from a bullying situation

- Get support from bystanders

- Improve their own self-esteem, and

- Remain calm when bullying begins.

The procedures are long and involved but they are highly effective. Readers who wish to pursue this as a strategy to be 'sold to' schools should read the relevant chapter in Sharpe and Smith (1994). A number of potentially useful sub-strategies are incorporated within this including strategies for responding to name-calling such as 'fogging', gaining the support of bystanders who otherwise become colluders, relaxation methods and 'stress inoculation', such as visualisation techniques. All of these have proven effectiveness and their presence in one single programme design is helpful and should be recommended to schools.

Other Within-School Strategies

There are many other effective strategies that school staff should be aware of although they do not have the significance and priority of those described above. The resource list in Appendix A covers many of them.

3. Prevention of Bullying

Bullying in the School Grounds: Studies throughout the world have shown that for children in the junior school years the most common location for within-school bullying is the playground and relatively unsupervised areas such as the surroundings of service buildings (e.g. boiler houses, kitchens, maintenance sheds).

There is little point in adopting elaborate within-school strategies to alleviate bullying if little or nothing is done to prevent the bullying that occurs throughout the grounds of the school. It is often claimed that what is required to end bullying outside the school building is greater supervision and headteachers have frequently made the point that the use of untrained playground supervisors at lunchtimes has led to a great increase in the amount of aggression. Yet many researchers (e.g. Boulton, 1994) make the point that bullying is such a complicated social behaviour that it is simplistic to believe that bullying will be eradicated by improving supervision. One reason is that some of the most common forms of bullying are not physically assaultive and therefore less likely to be observed by supervisors no matter how well trained they may be. Name-calling, for example, which can be devastating if it takes place over a long period, may appear to be nothing more than active conversation to playground supervisors 50 or 60 yards away.

However, the status of playground supervisors is not respected by pupils and in a consequence there is unlikely to be an inhibition of bullying behaviour in the long term on the basis of the discipline offered by them. Many of them, unlike the teachers in the school, live in the same streets as their pupils, their family backgrounds are well known and the parents of children frequently say they are not teachers and that their kids do not have to do what they say. It is necessary that schools should take action to improve the status of supervisors and other non-teachers whenever possible.

Playground bullying is not, however, just a matter of staffing and staff status. Bullying in and around the playground takes place for a myriad of other reasons and would do so even if the playground was staffed by the most efficient teachers in the school. Over the years of research a number of factors have been found to be most important:

- The size of the playground and the number of children who have to use it; small spaces and large numbers equals bullying;

- Marginalisation through games activities; large boys in primary playgrounds tend to dominate with games of football that take most of the space leaving the majority of children bored and restless at the periphery;

- Exclusion by labelling; children who are not deemed to be valuable in playground sporting activities are frequently excluded in a hostile fashion;

- The presence of children with physical and/or learning difficulties; these are antecedents to bullying in relatively unsupervised settings (Sharpe and Smith, 1994);

- 'Blind spots'; these are difficult to supervise areas. Such areas are well known to bullies who congregate near them;

- The social ethos of the school which may be poor due to authoritarian and coercive management, inadequate resources, scruffy and decaying appearance;

- Boredom and associated frustration.

There have been many studies on the school environment and its modification with the objective of reducing bullying and the Implementation Group need to be familiar with the best of these. At the present time the best descriptions for studying, describing and redesigning the school environment are provided by Michael Boulton and Catherine Higgins as two chapters in the Sharpe and Smith book.

Establishing School and Local Education
Authority Anti-Bullying Policies

The schools in the target community may have already put anti-bullying policies in place. Also the Local Education Authority responsible for them may have its own anti-bullying policy which covers all of its educational institutions. It is not often the case, however, that both of these are true, indeed the majority of Local Education Authorities and schools do not as yet have detailed policies in place. There is, however, a requirement in law that all schools shall protect their pupils and recently the Department for Education has been issuing guidelines about bullying. Increasingly such policies are extensions of good practice guidance about discipline and of equal opportunities but is it important to make sure that these extensions are not 'also rans' that create the impression that bullying is very much an after thought.

Policies are statements guiding organisations and action within an institution. An anti-bullying policy will set out in a statement of intent of what is to be achieved and how. The Local Education Authority policy has much the same characteristics and are designed to guide what happens in all the institutions that the Authority is responsible for. In order to implement policies, schools and colleges have to define the resources and processes available to prevent and ameliorate bullying. They will contain guidance to help staff learn more about the problem and how they should consistently and positively respond to it.

It is clear that such a policy will not be effective without the total and unequivocal support of the senior management. In respect of schools this means the headteacher and deputies, heads of departments, heads of years and other senior staff. With regard to local education authorities, the director and deputies must be seen to give an anti-bullying policy their fullest support, not just within the administration itself but also to the parents and pupils that they serve. Breaches of the policy should be dealt with quickly and positively by senior management who should seize every opportunity to remind all staff that the policy is valued and important.

The Structure of Anti-Bullying Policy Development: Sharpe and Thompson (1994) state that the process of policy development follows five distinct stages which are:

• Awareness-raising

• Confrontation

• Preparation of draft and transition of final policy

- Communication and implementation

- Maintenance and review.

They believe that the work done in formulating the policy is as important as its final content and implementation. This cannot be emphasised too much in relation to community anti-bullying projects where not only the schools' staff are involved, but also a substantial number of people, including parents, outside of the school. It is vital that they are part of a policy development process so that their awareness and strategic skills can grow at the same rate as those of the teachers and other professionals involved.

Previous chapters have already dealt with the processes of awareness raising within schools and within the community itself. The bully audits in the schools and community are a vital part of this process. The discussions which take place after the bully audits have been carried out will create a consultative atmosphere and the various professional, voluntary and parent representatives that have been nominated for the Implementation Group will provide the core personnel for the consultative process. As far as schools within the targeted community are concerned the governors and parents must be consulted fully for the Local Education Authority policy development must include local elected representatives as well as a wide range of people from statutory and voluntary agencies, and parent representatives. The work of these various groups should be made known to the community at large through the media and also through schools' newsletters, personal letters to parents and the local radio if possible. The details of such processes have already been discussed.

The Draft Policy: At the same time as the consultation has been ongoing, the schools, guided by the Implementation Group, will have been working on the anti-bullying strategies outlined in the first two sections of this chapter. The outcome of these strategies and the awareness that will have been raised by their implementation can be added to the outcome of consultation such that the whole data can be brought together and translated into a draft policy. This will, in its turn, go out for consultation. It may seem peculiar but the draft policy and its supporting procedures for a school will necessarily be more complex than that for a whole local education authority. The reason for this is that local education authorities may create policies which have to be implemented by the school in the best way that the teachers can. The local authority officers can, therefore, reasonably expect the school staff themselves to evolve the best strategies for implementing the policy.

In drafting the policy it is wise to work to a fairly tried and tested format by writing to a number of headings:

• Aims and objectives of the policy

• A definition of bullying

• What forms does bullying take (in relation to particular schools it is wise here to draw out information from the audit to describe the most prevalent forms of bullying in that immediate catchment area)

• How bullying may be recognised

• Prevention strategies

• Recording and reporting incidents of bullying

• Strategies for dealing with bullying

• Roles and responsibilities of all relevant parties

• Monitoring, evaluating and refining policies and procedures

Sharpe and Thompson (1994) provide a series of guidelines which underpin many of these headings but previous material should provide sufficient guidance.

An example of a detailed local educational authority anti-bullying policy is given in Appendix A of this chapter.

Communicating and Launching the Policy: Whilst at the draft stage it is necessary to open up consultations in order to encourage a wide audience to examine what is proposed and modify it if necessary. It is important that teachers from schools who are about to finalise their policy should go to schools that have already had one in place for some time in order that the possibilities of error are minimised and tested strategies for implementation are obtained.

The policy can be launched once consultations are over and agreed changes have been made. If a number of schools within the targeted community have arrived at this stage together then it is sensible to have a big media 'splash' and an official launch ceremony attended by local dignitaries and the media. Where schools are, however, working by themselves it is still desirable that the local media are asked to publicise the implementation of the new policy. With regard to local educational authorities it is important that whatever publicity machine is available should be utilised to maximum advantage. The object of having a big launch is to tell as many adults as possible and their children, that bullying will not be tolerated and that something is being done about it. One of the clearest messages that must be given is that parents are as responsible as schools for tackling bullying; they may be the immediate cause of bullying in schools and it is their responsibility to work closely with teachers to prevent matters from getting worse and ultimately to eradicate bullying from the school and its catchment.

Group Two: The Link Group
Introduction
The function of linking strategies is to bind together the anti-bullying initiatives taking place in the schools with those taking place in the community. Schools have always found it hard to engage with their catchment communities in a consistent and a business like way and that is also true in the reverse. Where large schools are concerned the problems of communication bedevil attempts to improve relationships and to work in harmony, not just with parents but the various institutions and agencies that function within the catchment community. This section focuses on what schools can do to establish better links with parents and other members of the community. The assumption is made that the Implementation Group has already laid the foundations for the strategies by bringing together representatives from all sides on to this group and to have prepared the way for this initiative through the media and other means of local communication.

Giving Information
As shown bullying is a secret activity, bullies do not want to be caught and victims are often too ashamed to tell. The secretiveness of the problem is the worst enemy of victims; if they could help themselves they would. Yet those adults who could possibly help them may never get to learn that their children, pupils or neighbours' children are suffering in this way. In the case of adults, the problem is even worse; adults are not expected to be victims, if they are then, in the minds of many people around them, they are weak, unable to stand up for themselves or possibly even attention seeking. Whatever the reasons that society gives for its inability to protect people against the worse excesses of aggression from bullies, one good way forward is to provide clear, user-friendly information about the signs of bullying that may be present when victims are unwilling to talk openly of their experiences and their fears.

The best way of conveying this information is through facts sheets. These can be arranged through local free papers, parish magazines, sponsored by companies such as major DIY stores who use mail shots, local radio and notes home to parents. If we concentrate solely on 'symptoms' shown by children then the information given in Appendix B is useful and has prompted many referrals to anti-bullying projects.

The 'bullying signs' lists for adults is naturally rather different yet close examination will reveal similar patterns and motivations. 'Symptoms' include (Adams, 1992):

Physical signs including

 Feeling sick before going to work and at work
 Shaking and sweating
 Sleep disturbance
 Palpitations
 Loss of energy
 Overactive stomach/bowels
 Bad headaches
 Strange aches and pains

Emotional signs including

 Anxiety
 Quick iritation
 Panic feelings / attacks
 Depression
 Anger/rage
 Reduced motivation
 Low self-confidence
 Low self-esteem
 Growing sense of isolation
 Deteriorating close relationships

Engaging Those Who Can Observe Bullying in the Community
A crucial link strategy has already been mentioned, namely the enlistment of shop workers, office workers and any other people working in the community who have the opportunity to observe bullying. Although the common trend is to feel guilty but do nothing about such activity it is quickly possible to engage such people in a simple reporting mechanism whereby named staff in schools can be alerted to what is happening to pupils out in the streets. The writer has found it useful to embark on a 'Bully Watch', paralleling the well known anti-crime initiative 'Neighbourhood Watch' because this captures the imagination of people who prefer to do their

fighting against bullying anonymously. The Bully Watch initiative can be launched in blaze of publicity and will attract local sponsorship. Parent groups can be used to do the leg work provided that they have a clear written brief and simple strategy.

Quality Circles

A growing number of people working in British industry familiar with quality circles (QC's). The idea comes from the armaments industry in America during the Second World War and has been taken up subsequently by Japanese industry where it was turned into an extremely effective linking strategy between management and shop floor. British industry has taken note of this and over the last 15 years Quality Circles have become a well established part of British employee/employer relations. Not surprisingly, educationalists have witnessed the startling effect that QCs have had on such relations and have worked hard to put them into the schools framework. In the context of bullying an excellent description is given by Cowie and Sharpe (1992) where the QC typically consists of groups of people, usually around five or six pupils, who get together regularly after training by a QC experienced person, to identify, describe and resolve problems. QC skills include analysis, solution forming and presentation of solutions to higher management. Elsewhere, for example in Norway, QCs may involve adults as well as children and it is not uncommon to find that parents are regular members and governors may be coopted on a fairly frequent basis. The QC group reports the outcomes of their discussions back to management. The book by Sharpe and Smith (1994) devotes a substantial part of its fourth chapter to a detailed and excellent description of establishing QCs in schools. This is essential reading for the Implementation Group and the establishment of such groups within the target area schools must be a priority.

The QC format presented by Cowie and Sharpe (1992, 1994) has a highly structured format:

- Establishing the QC group;

- Specifying problems and brainstorming them;

- Prioritising;

- Investigating prioritised problems and doing such research to detail them as is necessary;

- Identifying causes and antecedents;

- Suggesting solutions;

- Presenting the problems and their proposed solutions to management;

- Monitoring the problems and evaluating outcomes of intervention.

Smith and Sharpe (1994) emphasise the range of skills which the participants acquire in working through the QC format. These skills facilitate a problem-solving approach to social life and they actively discourage behaviour which is discriminatory or dominating. The QC approach is democratic and encourages trust and teamwork. Cowie and Ruddock (1990) suggest that group members are enabled through debriefing and regular group evaluation sessions to become acquainted with useful techniques in conflict resolution.

From the viewpoint of the community approach format becomes much more powerful when it also involves parent representatives and others, from the community. Not only do the pupils in the QCs have the opportunity to relay to non-teaching adults from outside of the school their proper concerns about bullying which takes place in the community but also it gives members of the community a greater sense of urgency about this behaviour. Children are their own best advocates. It is recommended, therefore, that the Implementation Group encourages each school to establish two or more QCs with specific reference to bullying that involve parent representatives, governors, employees and employers from within the community and others (for example, police liaison officers). It is further recommended that the outcomes of QC meetings are minuted and that these minutes are used to provide brief summary reports which are fed back into the community for the information of its members. The writer has found this to be a powerful linking strategy and, although the names of bullies and their families are not mentioned, it quickly becomes apparent who regular offenders are within the community and peer-pressures soon inhibit their excesses.

Group Three: Community Strategies(1)
Introduction
These strategies are those which are suitable for action in the community which schools may support but do not 'own'. The primary aim of these strategies is to improve the socialisation of individuals and so diminish inter-personal aggression of all sorts. Such strategies must be reactive, in that they respond to existing levels of bullying, and also proactive, in that to prevent poor levels of socialisation in the future. This particular aspect

of the project carries with it the best possibilities for long term success in reducing bullying. It is based upon the material presented in chapter two which show how roots of aggression and bullying are sown by faulty parenting styles during the pre-school years. The main thrust of these strategies is to work with parents to help them socialise their children. Before this aspect of the project is described it is first necessary to review the legal framework available to parents to help them in their attempts to prevent bullying. Knowing that the law is there to help them can give them greater confidence in this work.

Where the Law Stands on Bullying

Many members of the community are not aware that even if bullying is on school grounds, there may well be a case for prosecution. Not surprisingly schools are reluctant to involve police in matters of bullying because to most teachers these are matters for internal disciplinary action and of private rather than public reprisal. Yet the Implementation Group will soon find from people that schools are not always effective in reducing bullying and that in many cases parents complain that little or nothing is being done other than 'sweep the problem under a carpet'. Bullying often involves a criminal offence and the victims are entitled to the protection of the law usually by first calling in the police, whether or not the school agrees to their involvement.

The situation is a lot clearer when the bullying occurs outside of schools. Under such circumstances teachers and governors are less likely to try and persuade parents not to involve the police and may even encourage them. Many parents are often reluctant to take this step because they feel that the police are too busy or will not take them seriously or that other members of the community will think of them as informers. These attitudes often arise from ignorance of the law and a fact sheet can be really useful in empowering parents to take action. This sheet should not merely present a brief description of the facts but should also give examples of how ordinary people have been able to use the law to resolve severe difficulties of bullying. The content of such a sheet may contain material like this:

> Although bullying is not recognised as a criminal offence, the actions of the bully at specific times may well be criminal assault under the Offences Against the Person Act of 1861, and justify prosecution. The following examples are of cases where successful prosecutions took place. Notice how the assault can be direct or indirect. There does not have to be a physical injury for an act of bullying to be classed as assault.

- **Example One**: Simon, a 14 year old boy, was badly beaten up for a second time by a gang of known bullies at his Youth Club. He suffered a broken nose, fractured cheekbone and badly swollen right eye. His parents took him to the casualty department where the Doctor took X-rays, facial photographs and made copious notes all of which were subsequently used in the prosecution. Far from being called police informers the parents received many good wishes from other parents in the community saying how pleased they were that finally someone had the 'guts' to take action. Simon also received some compensation for his injuries.

- **Example Two**: Mandy, aged 11, was badly scared by a threatening group of boys from another school on her way home at 4 o'clock one winter's afternoon. When they ran at her, she became desperate, panicked and fell down a slippery railway embankment which caused a fractured right leg. Her father called in the police who quickly found three witnesses of the incident. A successful prosecution ensued and the parents received many congratulatory messages from others whose children had been intimidated by this group.

- **Example Three**: Jane, a 16 year old bully, made a series of threatening phone calls to thirteen year old Becky who had won a prize for dancing much coveted by Jane. Over a period of weeks Becky became more and more morose and eventually her father was able to establish what was happening; he reported the matter to Becky's headteacher who brought in his friend, a police liaison officer. This officer arranged a telephone tap. Jane was quickly trapped and prosecuted.

- **Example Four**: Rachel, a 14 year old black girl, was subject to severe racial bullying taking the form of name-calling and threats of mutilation. Unbeknown to her parents and teachers this had carried on for a period of nearly two years before she became so distressed that secondary anorexia developed and she became unable to attend school. Her friends eventually were persuaded to testify against the group and the oldest was prosecuted.

- **Example Five**: David, aged 15, was the regular victim of a group of bullies who had assaulted him on more than one occasion, destroyed his work and belongings and generally made his life hell. He had moderate learning difficulties and this was the catalyst for the prolonged efforts of the bullies against him. He did not complain about his treatment and his parents were unable to determine why he was losing weight, had sleepless nights and cried before going to school. They suspected he might have been bullied but it was only when a neighbour saw the bullying group dismantling his bike and hiding it that the true circumstances of his case came to light. A police liaison officer was involved and a successful prosecution followed on the grounds that tampering with the bike was liable to cause injury or death.

All these examples show assault or threaten assault in some form or another. This includes injury to another person's state of mind although that can be difficult to prove. Where bullying involves theft, as in extortion, then witnesses make prosecution much easier. Parents should be aware that this is true of theft occurring in schools as it is outside them.

Not all bullies will be prosecuted. It generally depends on how old they are. A child under ten years cannot be tried for a criminal offence and so is immune to prosecution. Persistently aggressive and dangerous children may, however, be taken into local authority care. Children in the 10-14 age group may be tried and found guilty of a criminal offence provided that it can be shown that the child was aware that they were doing something wrong. Such trials take place in the Juvenile Courts and the penalties frequently include such things as enforced supervision and counselling. From 14-17, bullies are still classified as juveniles but they are expected to understand their responsibility for any criminal behaviour they commit. The law also does not allow the defence that they didn't realise they were breaking the law. Such trials continue to take place in a Juvenile Court but extremely dangerous young people may be subject to a custodial sentence.

Group Three: The Community Strategies (2)
Work with the Parents of School Children

The material of chapter two shows how the roots of bullying are often laid down during a child's pre-school years. A community anti-bullying project should engage with the parents of such children to function in a preventative way to reduce the frequency and severity of bullying later on. The key to this work lies in a conceptualisation of child development whereby all developmental skills, perception, cognition, motor co-ordination and social understanding are inextricably linked. To work towards a goal of maximum development will obviously improve a child's chances of successful development in all areas.

One of the most successful ways of working with pre-school children is through playgroups and nurseries and encourage parents to take an active part in the work done. One very successful project not only established a playgroup of its own in the most deprived area of the targeted community but also worked extensively with other playgroups and nursery units. At the heart of this work was a 'parenting pack' (Randall, 1993) which provided a developmental curriculum in which good socialisation was linked to traditional developmental activities designed to stimulate children across the full range of developmental skills.

This pack was made available to every parent with pre-school children and it became the focal point of the preventative work. Even parents who had problems with literacy were able to access this user friendly pack and so could carry on with the activities at home. Parents were encouraged to form their own empowerment groups and establish their own control over the use of the pack. It was heartening to see how, in this deprived area, many of the parents who have been 'written off' by professional agencies as unworkable, found a role and responsibility within even the most complex of the activities. They supported each other, designed excellent modifications and came to show a pride in the 'good manners' of their small children.

Pre-School Intervention

It is unfortunate that the pre-school preventative work described above uncovers many children who, before they enter full time education, are already extremely aggressive and take pleasure in hurting other children. These youngsters will enter school as bullies unless there is some intervention to modify their behaviour. The project staff may be able to achieve this without support from outside agencies. The telecounselling and counselling services may be able to help parents make the necessary changes to behaviour management that are generally required when young children are producing aggressive behaviour on a regular basis. This is highly skilled work, however, and may be best left to other agencies such as the child guidance services run by local education authorities. It is therefore of the utmost importance that the Implementation Group has a good relationship with these services.

Information to Parents on the Pre-School Environment

Several studies from around the western world have shown how a poor pre-school playgroup, nursery or childminding service can lead to a number of undesirable behaviours including impulsive aggression from pre-school children. The community anti-bullying project should therefore help parents to understand what kind of environment they should be looking for when they submit their child to pre-school experiences. The following comments can help this process.

- *Named worker*: A named worker is someone who is specifically responsible for individual children. The name of this worker is given to parents as the child enters the group and is the main person to whom the parent would refer any concerns.

- *Degree of supervision*: Whilst there are fairly strict regulations laid down concerning the adult: child ratio there is little use to this if, as Sarah Lawson (1994) points out in her book for parents, the allegedly supervising adults are somewhere in a huddle chattering together. When parents visit a playschool, playgroup or nursery they should look carefully at the way in which adults are functioning. They should be visible within the group of children and not elsewhere working on tasks independently of those children.

- *The Environment*: Although many excellent playgroups take place in dingy church halls and prefabricated buildings there is no excuse for the interiors to be dull and boring. Broken toys should be picked up immediately and put away pending repair or disposal, there should be well mounted displays of children's work that are not covered with the dust of ages and there should be no obvious dangers. Examining equip-ment is also important; paint should be freshly made up, crayons not broken down into tiny stubs that small fingers can't grasp and pencils should be regularly Sharpened. Jigsaws should be kept in their boxes and not in a great intermingled pile.

- *Staff Discipline*: Gross inconsistencies often create problems for pre-school children by giving them mixed and confusing messages. Staff members who smile benignly at them one day only to scream at them in anger the next for the same behaviour are a danger no matter how well intentioned they are. If staff fail to keep the older and larger children under proper control then smaller ones will be distressed by a high level of random activity and noise. The staff should be aware of simple but clear rules for dealing with disagreements and there should be no need for them ever to shout at or nag children. The very worst punishment should be something like a 'naughty chair' in a quieter area of the group. This can be very helpful for children who are angry and upset and give them the opportunity to calm down with-out spreading their distress amongst the group. This chair should, however, be supervised at all times.

- *Staff Relationships*: There should be a happy business-like relation-ship between the members of staff. The group leader should show a clear sense of leadership and authority but be able to do this in a friendly and positive fashion. Comments from other parents who have had children in the group for some time will certainly indicate whether the staff work happily together. If they don't, then at times it is inevitable that their anger with each other will be transmitted to the children.

- *Staff involvement:* Staff who allow children to pick and choose, do what they like when they like, are useless as far as promoting development is concerned. The pre-school years are a time when children need structured experiences in order to help them move up the developmental ladder. Although they do learn a great deal from discovery as a consequence of their own actions it is also true that they discover very little unless the activities set out 'nudge' them in appropriate directions. Staff must be there to set out such activities properly and also to involve themselves with the children as they work with the materials. Staff who are standing around chatting to each other and parents are not involved with children and will allow bad 'work' habits to develop. These include poor attention control, weak span of concentration, inability to listen to instructions and partake in turn-taking activities. Such bad habits at infant level are the bain of every reception teacher's life when these children enter compulsory education.

- *Positive reinforcement for children*: One of the ways in which pre-school children come to be aggressive and bullying is associated with the lack of respect for them from adults. This includes parents and adults who supervise them in child care circumstances. To demonstrate respect for young children is a simple thing, it means no more than praising them, encouraging their efforts and being pleased with their best work (no matter how relatively weak that may be). Conversely it is as easy to show disrespect for a child by being disparaging and unhelpful. Parents should listen carefully to the comments made by staff to children in pre-school groups. There is a great difference between one who looks at a child attempting to use a posting box and says 'No, silly, that doesn't go there, it goes here' and one who says 'Ooh, You are trying really hard, I wonder if it might go up here' followed by a quick accurate gesture.

Similarly, comments from staff about poor behaviour are also very important. A member of staff who derides the child rather than the behaviour shows no respect and is likely to create resentment. Conversely, a member of staff who talks only about the behaviour and not the child is unlikely to create such an emotion. Thus, a member of staff who says 'You are a horrible nasty little boy for hurting Sally like that' and does so on a regular basis, will do far more damage to a child's self-esteem and social development than one who says 'I don't like behaviour like that, Sally is very upset now. What can you do to make her happy again?'

Community Support Systems

There are a variety of support systems that can be established to meet the needs of young people. Many children and young people will not talk to adults about their experiences of bullying but will talk to their peers. The following strategies can be established by the Implementation Group to provide for them.

Peer Counselling: Essentially adolescent volunteers are given basic counselling skills and are provided with facilities in which to meet victims. This service is then advertised widely around the schools in the catchment area and through the local media. It always helps if the local newspaper runs a case study based on the experiences a particular victim had with their peer counsellor. A good exposition of peer counselling and the necessary training is given by Robinson et al. (1991).

Buddying: This is a technique described in the 'That's Life' anti-bullying information pack sent to all schools. Not only does this enable younger children to be counselled but also befriended by older pupils who are in a position to protect them at times of greatest risk of bullying. This is one of the best ways of ensuring a victim's security at school.

Assertiveness Training for Adolescents and Adults: In previous chapters the possibility of assertiveness training was raised as a powerful antidote to bullying. After such training regular victims will have the assertiveness skills necessary for them to 'refuse' to be bullied. The Implementation Group should seriously consider establishing within the community a number of assertiveness groups for which recipients could pay a small fee to help sustain that particular part of the programme. What is trained should include the following (Clarke and Underwood, 1988):

- *Active listening/reflecting listening skill*: This is a mode of response to people involving the listener in reformulating and returning the speaker's (bully's) utterances. This mode focuses on the speaker's intended meaning without judgment and analysis or any tendency on the listener's part to impute a personalised interpretation. This is a 'trouble defusing' technique in that it avoids misunderstandings (by providing the opportunity for meaning to be checked), shows exceptance of the speaker (through empathy — often hard to do when the speaker is a bully) rather than criticism and allows the speaker to retain 'ownership' of the problem. This latter is particularly important in the case of adult bullies because, in a very real sense, it directs their bullying comments back at them. Reflective listening has a calming effect because speakers of vitriolic and bullying utterances are confronted with their own words being delivered back to them in a calm and non-threatening way.

- *Persuasion skill through the 'broken record'*: This is the ability to persuade others to see and agree with a point of view, expressed clearly and without losing self-possession. One of the strategies to learn is how to keep bringing stressful conversations back to a point by continuous repetition of that point. This prevents bullying individuals from diverting their attacks into other areas where they may have more success.

- *Handling criticism*: This is the ability to deal with personal criticism in a way which does not involve losing self-esteem. There are a number of tactics which were of use within this. Fogging, for example, is a means by which people receive personal criticism without becoming defensive or upset. They may make comments back to the offensive party such as 'Well, that might be your point of view'. Such a technique helps in avoiding confrontation by appearing to accept the criticism in a non-aggressive manner without causing further provocation or losing self-esteem. Another unrelated technique is known as Negative Enquiry where the listener simply asks for more information from the bully. The bullyies are put into a position of having to defend comments which they have probably said just to hurt without having any real substance. The result may be consternation and surprise allowing the intended victim to move on with no sense of loss.

- *Giving and receiving feedback*: At times it is useful for intended victims to give simple direct feedback to the potential bully. The heart of this is a series of 'I' statements rather than 'you' statements. So instead of saying 'You are upsetting me' the intended victim could say 'OK, I take your point — such as it is' and walk on without further conversation. Such an approach does not provide the distressed emotional response the bully really wants but, at the same time, is not highly provocative. At times the bully may well make statements about the intended victims behaviour that are instructive because they demonstrate particular traits of the victim's behaviour that encourages bullying. This kind of feedback can be useful because the intended victims can to re-appraise their behaviour and make changes as necessary.

- *Non-verbal communication*: It is important that 'body language', a vital form of non-verbal communication behaviour, is consistent with what is said such that the one supports the other preventing contradictory messages. Tone of voice, gestures, posture and eye contact are faithful reflections of inner feelings and can be just as reinforcing to the bullies who witness the fear they provoke through these obvious signs of distress.

APPENDIX A
Community Anti-bullying Project Resource List

Anti-bullying materials to facilitate school policy development

Besag, V. (1992) *We Don't Have Bullies Here!*, Available from V. Besag, 57 Manor Road, Jesmond, Newcastle-upon-Tyne, NE2 2LY.

Islington Safer Cities Project (1990) *We Can Stop It!* London: Islington Safer Cities Project. A resource pack supplemented by a video.

Johnstone, M., Munn, P. and Edwards, C. (1992) *Action against Bullying,* The Scottish Council for Research in Education.

Randall, P.E. and Donohue, M.J. (1994) *The Prevention of School Based Bullying*, Hull: FASU, University of Hull.

Tattum, D.P. and Herbert, G. (1990), *Bullying: A Positive Response*, Faculty of Education, South Glamorgan Institute of Higher Education, Cyncoed Road, Cardiff, CF2 6XD.

Thompson, D. and Sharp, S. (1994), *Establishing Whole School Policies on Pastoral Issues*, London: David Fulton.

Materials Guiding School Responses to Bullying

Arora, C.M.J. (1991), The use of victim support groups. In P.K. Smith and D. Thompson (eds). *Practical Approaches to Bullying*. London: David Fulton.

de Silva, C. and Ross, C. (1991) *I can Look After Myself?* London: Islington Educational Authority.

Elliot, M. (1991) *Bullying: A Practical Guide to Coping in Schools*. Harlow: Longman.

Maines, B. and Robinson, G. (1991) *Stamp Out Bullying*, Bristol: Lame Duck Publishing.

Maines, B. and Robinson, G. (1992) *Michael's Story: The No Blame Approach*. Bristol: Lame Duck Publishing.

Pikas, A. (1989) The common concern method for the treatment of mobbing. In E. Roland and E. Munthe (eds) *Bullying: An International Perspective*, London: David Fulton.

Working on High-Risk Areas in Schools

Adams, E. (1990) *Learning through landscapes: a report on the design management and development of school grounds.* Winchester: Learning Through landscapes Trust.

Blatchford, P. and Sharp, S. (1993) *Breaktime and The School: Understanding and Changing Playground Behaviour*. London Routledge.

DES (1990) The outdoor classroom: educational use, Landscape design and management in school grounds, *Building Bulletin*, 71, London: HMSO.

Imich, A. and Jeffries, K. (1989) Management of Lunchtime Behaviour, *Support for Learning*, 4, 46-52.

OPTIS (1986) *Lunchtime Supervision*, Oxfordshire Programme for Training, Oxford: Oxfordshire County Council.

Ross, C. and Ryan, A. (1990) *Can I Stay in Today, Miss? — Improving The School Playground*, Stoke-on-Trent: Trentham.

Sahrp, S. and Smith, P.K. (1993) Making changes to playtime, *Topic,* Windsor: NFER-Nelson.

Curriculum Materials

Brown, C. Barnfield, J. and Stone, M. (1990) *Spanner in the works: Education for Racial Equality and Social Justice in White Schools.* Stoke-on-Trent: Trentham.

Casdagli, P., Gobey, F. and Griffin, C. (1990) *Only Playing, Miss.* Stoke-on-Trent: Trentham. Script and drama ideas.

Elliot, M. (1986) *Willow Street Kids.* London: Andre Deutschj.

Elliot, M. (1993) *The bullies meet the Willow Street kids.* London: Pan Macmillan Children's Books.

Gibbon, F. (1991) *Chicken,* London: Dent Children's Books.

Gobey, F. (1991) A practical apporach through drama and workshops. In P.K. Smith and D. Thompson (eds). *Practical Approaches to Bullying.* London: David Fulton.

Godden, R. (1991) *The Diddakoi.* London: Pan.

Golding, W. (1954) *Lord of the Flies.* London: Faber and Faber.

Grunsell, A. (1989) *Lets Talk About Bullying,* London: Gloucester Press.

Hill, S. (1974) *I'm the King of the Castle* Harmondsworth: Penguin.

Housden, C. (1991) The use of the theatre workshops and role play in PSE in a secondary school. In P.K. Smith and D. Thompson (eds) *Practical Approaches to Bullying* London: David Fulton.

Kumar, A. (1985) *The Heartstone Odyssey* Allied House (The Heartsone Organisation can be contacted at Allied Mouse, First Floor, Longden Court, Spring Gardens, Buxton, Derbyshire SK17 68Z).

Maines, B. and Robinson, G. (1991) *Stamp Out Bullying* Bristol: Lame Duck Publications.

Ostler, A. (1989) *Speaking Out· Black girls in Britian,* London: Virago.

Books

Apart from those already listed the following are very useful:

Besag, V. (1989) *Bullies and victims in schools.* Milton Keynes: Open University Press.

Byrne, B. (1994), *Bullying: A Community Approach,* Dublin: Columba.

Canter, L. and Canter, M *Assertive discipline: Positive behaviour management for today's classroom.* London: Cassell

Casdagli, P. Cobey, F. and Griffin, C. (1990) *Only Playing Miss* Stoke-on-Trent: Trentham.

Commission for Racial Equality (1987) *Learning in Terror: A Survey of Racial Harrassment in Schools and Colleges in England, Scotland and Wales, 1985-1987,* London: CRE.

Derman-Sparks, L. *Anti bias curriculum: Tool for empowerment of young children* Washington: National Association for the Education of Young Children.

Elliot, M. (1992) *Bullying: a practical guide to coping for schools* Essex: Longman group.

Tattum, D. and Herbert, C. (1993) *Countering bullying — initiatives by Schools and Local Authorities* Stoke-on-Trent: Trentham.

Children's Books

Bryant-Mole, K. (1992) *What's happening?: Bullying* Sussex: Wayland.

Elliot, M. (1987) *The willow street kids* London: Pan Mcmillan

Elliot, M. (1993) *The bullies meet the willow street kids* London: Pan Mcmillan.

Elliot, M. *A safety guide for young children feeling happy, feeling safe* London: Hodder and Stoughton.

Freed, A. (1991) *T.A for tots and other prinzes* Los Angeles: Jlamir Press.

Freed, A. and Freed, M. (1991) *The new T.A for kids — development of self esteem* Los Angeles: Jlamir Press.

APPENDIX B

SHIRE COUNTY COUNCIL
EDUCATION SERVICES
ANTI-BULLYING POLICY STATEMENT

The Local Education Authority recognises that bullying takes place in a variety of ways and is abhorrent behaviour which can, in the long term, cause extreme distress and life-long psychological damage. There is no evidence that this area has a greater problem than other parts of the country.

The policy of the LEA is that although all educational establishments are encouraged to work to their own definition of bullying the operational definition for the purposes of the policy statement is that:

'Bullying is a pattern of behaviour that arises from group or individual victimisation with the intention of causing physical or psychological distress to others or to extort something from them'.

The policy of the LEA is that:

All educational establishments produce a policy statement and guidelines for dealing with bullying.

All educational establishments have in place carefully monitored procedures which are reviewed on an annual basis.

Copies of the guidelines should be given to all members of the school community/educational establishment.

All educational establishments should have a specifically identified member(s) of staff who will monitor all reported incidents of bullying.

All governors should note the legal duty of the governing body to safeguard the welfare of pupils.

The LEA will support the implementation of the policy and guidelines by providing a facilitator and appropriate resources.

GUIDELINES
SUGGESTED CONTENT FOR A PAMPHLET FOR PARENT

Partnership between parents and schools is recognised as being of crucial importance both in dealing with bullying and preventative work.

Fostering this partnership is an issue in most schools, this appendix offers you ideas that you might like to use in the preparation of a pamphlet for parents.

1   Introductory Ideas

You may like to draw attention to:

- the national concerns about the problems of bullying

- that there is no evidence that this area has a bigger problem of bullying than anywhere else in the Country;

- the recognition of the importance of partnership between parents and schools both to prevent and eradicate bullying;

- the importance of sharing with parents how your school has been studying the problem (definition/code of practice);

- the need to let parents know that the School Governors have been alerted to the problems of bullying if parents feel they need Governors help and support.

2   How can parents tell if their child is being bullied?

Bullying is often referred to as 'the silent nightmare' because many children (and quite a few adults) are too ashamed to admit that they are being bullied. On top of this bullying is a secretive activity — bullies do not take the risk of being spotted by anyone capable of stopping them.

There are signs of distress that almost shouts out 'I'm being bullied'.

Warning signs:

- not wanting to go to school;

- avoiding particular lessons or days;

- taking longer or different routes to and from school;

- very late for school, hanging back or returning late from school;

- avoiding friends and other children;

- having 'mystery illnesses' — non-specific pains, tummy upsets, head-aches;

- having unexplained cuts and bruises;

- torn and damaged clothing and belongings;

- 'mislaid' books, equipment and belongings;

- asking for extra pocket money or sweets without giving clear reasons;

- under-achievement;

- personality changes — irritable, withdrawn, tired, poor sleeping, weepiness, crying outbursts, loss of appetite, forgetfulness, distracti-bility;

- temper outbursts, abusive language, impulsive hitting out;

- lack of confidence, making excuses for not going out to play or meeting other children;

- nightmares;

- bed-wetting.

3 **What can parents do about bullying?**

- Discuss it with the child — do not ask straight out, 'is someone bullying you'; the shame associated with bullying is to do with the fact that the child cannot 'stick up for themselves'. Instead ask 'is anyone in your school being nasty to other children?' Listen carefully to the answers and try to get the name or names of children who bully other children.

- Sympathise, listen carefully and try to calmly ascertain the facts.

- Reassure the child that the bullying will stop.

- Try to help the child use it as a learning experience and to see it as a problem to be solved.

- If the bullying has been going on for a long time or is very unpleasant, go straight to the school and discuss it with the Headteacher or some other senior member of staff. (There may be a teacher who has special responsibility for this sort of problem).

- If the bullying is happening in school (and most bullying does happen during school hours), or on the way to and from school then try and work out a plan with the teacher for dealing with it.

- Start to keep a record of the incidents of bullying, listing WHO, WHEN, WHERE and HOW. This is a painful thing to do but it does provide good 'ammunition' if the bullying does not stop.

- It is better if the children can overcome the problem for themselves — that is without your direct and obvious help. If you do have to provide direct help, do it tactfully. So, for example, if you decide to collect your child from school do not linger outside the school gates; try and wait around the corner instead.

- Do not advocate a 'hit them back' policy. This may be alien to your child's temperament and may involve more shame or a great deal of pain if the bully is bigger and stronger.

   If, on the other hand, your child decides to fight back and subsequently gets into trouble for fighting, use the records you have been keeping to support and explain your child's behaviour.

- If the bullying is violent and occurs outside of school, let the bully's parents know what is happening, preferably through school. If the situation does not improve be prepared to contact a solicitor and ask for a letter to be sent to the bully's parents, informing them of the legal consequences.

4   How can children help themselves to avoid bullying?

If your child is being bullied or you are aware that bullying does go on in your area it is helpful to teach some basic strategies. it is best to warn and advise children how to cope well in advance.

This teaching should start with the strong message that bullying is very, very wrong and that the child should never feel ashamed to tell if they are being bullied. Please make sure that this message is completely understood.

- Always tell an adult you trust if you are bullied.

- Stay with your friends and all of you 'NO' to the bully. Remember, there is safety with other people; bullies are cowards who do not like to be watched.

- Avoid going into places where bullying happens; certainly do not go into them alone.

- Practice saying 'NO' to the bully. Speak slowly, clearly and firmly. It sometimes helps to rehearse this in front of a mirror.

- Try not to loose your temper; stay calm. Crying and running away often gives free entertainment. Look the bully in the eye, stand up straight, try to look confident and walk quietly away.

- Do not try to fight back if you know the bully with hurt you.

- Leave expensive things at home and do not boast about money or possessions. If you are asked for things try to make an excuse. If things are forced from you and you feel you cannot refuse, do not fight to get them back. Tell an adult the truth and ask for help as soon as you can.

- If you are bullied by being called a name, ignore them. The best that the bully can hope for is to see you get upset. Ignoring can be very difficult but try hard.

- Ask yourself if your behaviour is inviting bullying. Could you change your behaviour in any way?

The best strategy is not be alone in places where bullying flourishes. So encourage children to stay with friends and make sure they all support each other against bullying.

5   Other Factors

Unfortunately many bullies have aggressive or neglectful parents. These parents are not usually supportive of their children's victims or helpful to the parents of the victims. Some of them encourage their children, particularly their sons, to be tough 'macho' characters. They even gain some satisfaction from the complaints they receive.

They should learn that this is unacceptable so please do not dismiss the idea of taking legal advice.

Establishing a whole school response to bullying

CHECKLIST FOR A WHOLE SCHOOL APPROACH

1   Raising Awareness About Bullying

Survey the children and staff

- How should we make others aware of the issue of bullying? Do we need to make a written statement about bullying available to governors, parents, the support services?

- What about other staff in the school: welfare assistants, lunch time supervisors, caretakers, etc? How can they be made aware of the problem?

2   Knowledge About Bullying

- Do we know enough about bullying and the complexities associated with it?

- How should we record incidents of bullying? How can we get children to let us know when they are being bullied and by whom? What system should we have for encouraging parents to report their fears of bullying to us? How can we inform them of the signs of bullying; is a parent pack adequate for the purpose?

- Do we need to ask the support services about bullying and to be involved in assisting us in this project?

3   Current Methods of Reducing Bullying

- What do we do now to stop bullying? Does anyone know we do it, like the parents and governors? Do we all do it or only some of us? Are our methods used consistently throughout the school?

- Do we really listen to parents when they complain of bullying?

- Do we know what methods are successful in reducing bullying?

- Do we know what methods are successful in preventing bullying?

- Do some of us use intimidation (a form of bullying) as a means of discipline? Some pupils will imitate this behaviour.

- Do we make the mistake of 'bullying the bullies' when we discipline them? This simply teaches them that 'might is right'.

- Do some of us condone bullying by not dealing with it when it is drawn to our attention?

- Do some of us believe that bullying is something to be endured in order to learn 'to take the rough with the smooth'?

4 **Identifying Bullying 'Hot Spots'**

- Do we know where bullying occurs in the school? What can be done to supervise these areas more effectively? What about the use of parent volunteers? Can pupils help with supervision?

- What about bullying to and from school; do we need to have regular feedback from school-crossing staff, bus drivers and people living near the school?

- Do we need to train non-teaching staff in the practice of monitoring bullying (eg, lunch time supervisors)?

- Does the arrangement of furniture in some classrooms make for supervision blind spots that bullies can exploit?

5 **Dealing With Parents: The Essential Anti-Bullying Partnership**

- What can we do to help parents learn more about bullying; how can we teach them what to look out for?

- Should we regularly inform parents when their children are found to be victims/bullies? If so, who should do the informing and under what circumstances?

- How can we encourage parents to come to us if they suspect bullying? If we do manage to encourage them, how can we reduce 'false alarms' or deliberate mis-representation?

- What about instituting some kind of confidential reporting mechanism for anyone (including pupils) to inform us about bullying? Can parents' meetings that are routine (eg open evenings) help us with this or is the current level of bullying so bad that we need to call a special meeting with parents?

6 **Relationships With Other Schools**

- Are our pupils being bullied by children/young people from other schools? Is there a need for a whole pyramid response (there often is in areas of high density urban estate living such that a secondary school and its feeder primaries are all within a fairly small locality)?

- Have other schools tackled the problem of bullying? Can we use their ideas or profit from their experiences?

7 Informative Contacts with Support Agencies

- If we have a lot of bullies coming from aggressive homes can we use other agencies to tackle the problems of the parents (eg, Social Service, Child Guidance, voluntary agencies like Homestart)?

- Should we seek help or materials from other agencies that have experience of tackling bullying (eg, Community Anti-Bullying Project — Tel: 01482 858585)?

CURRICULUM IMPLICATIONS OF BULLYING

The only effective way of preventing bullying is to teach pupils from as early as age as possible that bullying is totally unacceptable.

Anti-bullying tactics must include curriculum inputs if young children are to acquire the understanding of why it is unacceptable and whey they must report it. It may be that you already have some kind of input but even if you have, the following discussion items may help to cement this teaching throughout the school.

1 Personal and Social Education

- Is there a group responsible for monitoring and designing PSE throughout the school? Should there be one to help coordinate curriculum inputs on bullying and relate them to other topics associated with care and concern for others?

- Can anti-bullying themes be woven into assemblies and other whole school occasions? What opportunities exist to discuss bullying?

- If the problem of bullying is bad, can anything be done to start social skills training exercises giving practice in dealing with bullies (eg, role play, drama, class discussion)?

- Can children be encouraged to support those who are being bullied (eg, by staying with them and jointly threatening to tell a teacher)?

- When is bullying referred to in lessons? In what way can cross-curricular themes be used to reinforce lessons about bullying?

- Does the multi-cultural curriculum deal adequately with the bullying issues associated with ethnic differences.

Appendix C

STRATEGIES USEFUL IN THE CONTROL OF BULLYING

STAFF INITIATED STRATEGIES

The best strategies are always those we work out ourselves. We own them and therefore we make them work. This is the thrust of whole school approaches, where staff develop the plans and systems by consensus and as a result achieve a greater sense of ownership and motivation.

The following strategies have been used successfully in a variety of settings so it is important to note, however, that there is no guarantee with any of these methods but if used consistently they will reduce the incidence of ongoing bullying.

General Comments

1. Make records of all incidents and let both bully and victim see that you are doing so. Hopefully your records should show a decrease in the bullying — if they do not then change your method.

2. Do not deal with bullies and victims separately. Give your pleasant attention to the victims but prevent them from trying to get their own back whilst you are there to support them. Do not force bullies to apologiste. Apologies made under duress are as worthless as confessions obtained by torture. All this does is to teach bullies that people who are bigger and stronger than they are can force them to do things they do not want to do; they know they are being bullied.

3. Praise bullies when they are being pleasant. If you have reason to believe that they are lacking in self-esteem and get little success from educational and other attainments then it will pay to praise them publicly and privately. If this is to work you should see evidence of progress within about three weeks.

4. Analyse the bullying situations carefully. You may find that a pattern of situations is revealed. It is then possible to separate bully from victim by the judicious use of activities. DO NOT keep them apart by moving one or other into different situations; this will not cause the bully to change his/her opinion of the victim. If possible, under close supervision, put them in the same work teams. Close cooperation often causes bullies to gradually re-appraise their opinions of victims. This method also helps the victim regain his self-esteem.

5. If the bullying occurs on the way home from school allow the victim to leave before the bullies. Never allow a gang of bullies to leave en masse.

6. Punishment is not usually a productive method of dealing with bullies; it just reinforces their view that big strong people can bully smaller ones. It may be

necessary to use punishment in the first instance if the bullying is particularly frequent or vicious. The best punishers are restitutional; the bullies have to make appeasement by some act of public service which, it is explained to them, is their way of caring for people that they have hurt.

7. The use of peer pressure is extremely effective. Tell the class that they can all have a special treat after one bully-free week (or shorter period if the pressure is intense). Make sure that there is no treat if the bully strikes! Explain to the class why they did get their treat and ask for their aid in helping the bully(ies) to give up bullying. Tell them to inform you that bullying is taking place so that you can stop it, this will earn them an additional treat. This method is very successful in stopping bullies from becoming even more secretive in their activities.

8. Some schools have used 'Bully Courts' to exert peer pressure. There are several variations of these but essentially they all create a mock 'court' with accused, accusers, judge and jury. Children take the various roles and their class teacher guides them through the process of weighing evidence and passing a verdict. The punishment may be set by the class with direction from the teacher.

9. Parent cooperation should always be sought; even the bully's parents should be notified. This is a matter of commonsense; if the bully ever has to be suspended the parents will not be in position to claim that they had never been given the chance to do something about it. In addition such parents can provide another form of reward system if you are able to send a note home saying that their child has made good efforts to behave well.

10. Extortion requires an additional input. Whatever may be used from the lists above, it is also necessary to introduce teaching about property rights. Restitutional punishment is also useful where bullies have to return the property they took or its equivalent value. Parents must always be involved.

11. Do not forget that persistent victims need some intervention as well. In order to improve poor levels of self-esteem, one possible method is 'jigsaw'.

This method requires that small groups are given a designated project to complete, matters are then arranged in order that the low status child has a particular responsibility for a key task, the teacher ensures covertly that the child completes this task well.

References

Adams, A., (1992) *Bullying at Work*, London: Virago.

Adams, R. (1990) *Self-help, Social Work and Empowerment*, London: Macmillan.

Als, H. (1986) A syntactic model of neonatal behavioral organisation, *Physical Occupational Therapy in Paediatrics*, 6, 3-53.

Armstrong, P. and Little, C. (1993) Needs assessment in Northern Ireland: Looking at the NARP experiment, N.H.S. *Management Executive News*, February 1993.

Askew, S. (1989) Aggressive behaviour in boys: To what extent is it institutionalised? In D.P. Tuttum and D.A. Lane (Eds.) *Bullying in Schools*, Stoke-on-Trent: Trentham.

Aspler, R., and Hoople, H. (1976) Evaluation of crisis services with anoymous clients, *American Journal of Community Psychology*, 4, 293-302.

Back, K. and Back, K. (1991) *Assertiveness at Work*, London: McGraw Hill.

Bandura, A. (1977) *Social Learning Theory*, New Jersey: Prentice Hall.

Bandura, A. Ross, D. and Ross, A. (1961) Transmission of aggression through imitation of aggressive models, *Journal of Abnormal Social Psychology*, 63, 575, 582.

Baumrind, D. (1967) Child care practices anteceding three patterns of preschool behaviour, *Genetic Psychology Monographs*, 75, 43-88.

Baumrind, D. (1971) Current patterns of parental authority, *Developmental Psychology Monographs*, 4, 28-47.

Billings, A.G. and Moos, R.H. (1985) Children of parents with unipolar depression: A controlled 1 year follow-up, *Journal of Abnormal Child Psychology,* 14, 149-166.

Birch and Russell (1983) *Power: A New Social Analysis*, New York : Norton.

Block, J.H., Block, J. and Morrison, A. (1981) Parental agreement-disagreement on child-personality correlates in children, *Child Development*, 52, 965-974.

Bloom, M., (1975) *The Paradox of Helping*, New York: John Wiley.

Boulton, M.J. (1994) Preventing and responding to bullying in the junior/middle school playground. In S. Sharp and P.K. Smith (eds) *Tackling Bullying in Your School: A Practical Handbook for Teachers.* London: Routledge.

Boulton, M.J. and Underwood, K. (1992) Bully/victim problems among middle school children, *British Journal of Educational Psychology*, 62, 73-87.

Bowers, L., Smith, P.K. and Binney, V. (1992) Cohesion and power in the families of children involved in bully/victim problems at school, *Journal of Family Therapy*, 14, 371-387.

Bowlby, J. (1973) *Attachment and loss: Separation, anxiety and anger*, New York: Basic Books.

Bradshaw, J. (1992) *The conceptualisation and measurement of need*, Paper for the ESRC seminar, University of Salford, 20 January 1992.

Brennan, P., Mednick. S. and Kandel, E. (1991) Congenital determinants of violent and property offending, in, D.J. Pepler and K.H. Rubin (eds) *The Development and Treatment of Childhood Aggression*, Hillsdale: Lawrence Erlbaum.

Bretherton, I. Fritz, J., Zahn-Waxler, C. and Ridgeway, D. (1986) Learning to talk about emotion: A functionalist perspective, *Child Development,* 57, 529-548.

Brendan, B. (1994) *Bullying: A Community Approach*, Dublin: Columbia.

Burgess, R.L. and Conger, R.D. (1977) Family interaction patterns related to child abuse and neglect: Some preliminary findings, *Child Abuse and Neglect*, 1, 269-277.

Burton, P. (1993) *Community Profiling: A Guide to Identifying Local Needs*, Bristol: University of Bristol.

Byrne, B. (1994) *Bullying: A Community Approach*, Dublin: Columba.

Campbell, S. (1990) *Behavioural Problems in Preschool Children: Clinical and Developmental Issue*, New York: Guilford.

Cairns, R.B., Cairns, B.D., Neckerman, H.J., Gest, S.D. and Gariépy, J.L. (1988) Social networks and aggressive behaviour: Peer support or peer rejection?, *Developmental Psychology*, 24, 815-823.

Campos, J., Barrett, K., Lamb, M., Goldsmith, H. and Stenberg, C. (1983) Socioemotional development, in, P.H. Mussen (ed.) *Handbook of Child Psychology* (Vol, 11) pp 793-916, New York: Wiley.

Campbell, S., Euring, L., Breaux, A., and Szumowski, E. (1986) Parent-referred problem three-year-olds: Follow-up at school entry, *Journal of Child Psychology and Psychiatry*, 27, 473-488.

Chazan, M. (1989) Bullying in the infant school. In D.P. Tattum and D.A. Lane (Eds.). *Bullying In Schools*. Stoke-on-Trent: Trentham.

Cicchetti, D., Cummings, E.M., Greenberg, M. and Marvin, R. (1990) An organizational perspective on attachment beyond infancy: Implications for theory, measurement and research, in, M. Cummings (eds) *Attachment in the Preschool Years*, Chicago: University of Chicago Press.

Ciccheti, D., Ganiban, J. and Barnett, D. (1990) Contributions from the study of high risk populations to understanding the development of emotion regulation, in, K. Dodge and J. Garber (eds) *The Development of Emotion Regulation*, New York: Cambridge University Press.

Clarke, D. and Underwood, J. (1988) *Assertion Training*, Cambridge: NEC.

Clarke, K.B., (1965) *Dark Ghettos: Dilemmas of Social Power*, New York: Harper and Rowe.

Conger, R.D., Conger, K.J., Elder, G.H., Lorenz, F., Simons, R. and Whitbeck, L. (1992) A family process model of economic hardship and adjustment of early adolescent boys, *Child Development*, 63, 526-541.

Cowie, H. and Ruddock, J. (1990) *Cooperative Living: Traditions and Transitions. BP Education*, PO Box 30, Blacknest Road, Blacknest, Alton, Hants GU34 4BR.

Cowie, H. and Sharp, S. (1992) Students themselves tackle the problem of bullying, *Pastoral Care in Education*, 10, 31-37.

Cowie, H. and Sharp, S. (1994) Tackling bullying through the curriculum. In S. Sharp and P.K. Smith (eds) *Tacking Bullying in Your School: A Practical Handbook for Teachers*. London: Routledge.

Cox, M.J., Owen, M., Lewis, J.M. and Henderson, V.K. (1989) Marriage, adult adjustment and parenting, *Child Development*, 60, 1015-1024.

Crawford, N. (1985) *Power and Powerlessness in Organisations*, London: Tavistock Clinic Paper No. 52, unpublished.

de Shazer, S. (1985) *Keys to Solution in Brief Therapy*, New York: W.W. Norton.

de Shazer, S. (1991) *Putting Differences to Work*, New York: W.W. Norton.

Dodge, K.A. and Frame, C.L. (1982) Social cognitive biases and deficits in aggressive boys, *Child Development*, 53, 620-635.

Doel, M. and Marsh, P. (1992) Task-centred social work, Chapter 2 in C. Harvey and T. Philpot, (eds.)., *Practising Social Work*, London: Routledge.

Dooley, D. and Catalano, J.C. (1988) Recent research on the psychological effects of unemployment, *Journal of Social Issues*, 44, 1-12.

Downey, G. and Coyne, J.C. (1990) Children of depressed parents: An integrative review, *Psychological Bulletin*, 108, 50-76.

Dunn, J. (1992) Siblings and development, Current Directions in *Psychological Science*, 1(1) 6-9.

Edgecumbe, R. and Sandler, J. (1974) Some comments on 'Aggression turned against the self', *International Journal of Psychoanalysis*, 55, 365-368.

Eggleston, J., Dunn, D. and Anjali, M. (1986) *Education for Some*, Stoke-on-Trent: Trentham.

Eisen, A., (1994) Survey of neighborhood-based, comprehensive community empowerment initiatives. *Health Education Quarterley*, 21, 235-252.

Eisenberg, N. and Mussen, P. (1989) *The Roots of Prosocial Behaviour in Children*, Cambridge: Cambridge University Press.

Emde, R. (1985) The prerepresentational self and its affective core, *Psychoanalytic Study of the Child*, 38, 165-192.

Enright, M.F. and Parsons, B.V., (1976) Training crisis intervention specialists and peer group counsellors as therepeutic agents in the gay community, *Community Mental Health Journal*, 12, 383-391.

Eron, L.D., Huesmann, L.R., Dubow, E., Romanoff, R. and Yarmel, P.W. (1987) Aggression and it correlates over 22 years. in, D.H. Gowell, I.M. Evans, and C.R.O'Donnell (eds.) *Childhood Aggression and Violences*, New York; Plenum.

Fagot, B. and Hagan, R. (1985) Aggression in toddlers: Response to the assertive acts of boys and girls, *Sex Roles*, 12, 341-351.

Flay, B.R. (1987) Mass media and smoking cessation: a critical review, *American Journal of Public Health*, 77, 153-160.

Flora, J.A. and Wallack, L. (1990) Health promotion and mass media use: translating research into practice, *Health Education Research*, 5, 73-80.

Fox, N. and Davidson, R. (1984) Hemisphere substrates of affect: A developmental model. In, N.A. Fox and R.J. Davidson (eds.) *The Psychology of Affective Development*, Hillsdale, N.J: Lawrence Erlbaum.

Freud, A. (1968) *Normality and Pathology in Childhood*, Middlesex: Penguin.

Frodi, A., Macauley, J. and Thorne, D.P. (1977) Are women less aggressive than men? A review of the experimental literature, *Psychological Bulletin*, 84, 634-666.

Frude, N. (1992) *Understanding Family Problems*, Chichester: John Willey.

Gelfand, D.M. and Teti, D.E. (1990) The effects of maternal depression on children, *Clinical Psychological Review*, 10, 329-353.

Gabel, S. and Shindledecker, R. (1993) Parental substance abuse and its relationship to severe aggression and antisocial behaviour in youth, *American Journal of Addiction* 2(1) 40-58.

Garofalo, J., Siegel, L. and Laub, J. (1987) School related victimizations among adolescents: An analysis of National Crime Surey (NCS) narratives, *Journal of Quantitative Criminology*, 3, 321-338.

Gibb, C. and Randall, P.E. (1989) *Professionals and Parents: Managing Children's Behaviour*, London: Macmillan.

Gilmartin, B.G. (1987) Peer group antecedents of severe love-shyness in males, *Journal of Personality*, 55, 467-489.

Greenberg, M.T. and Speltz, M.C. (1988) Contributions of attachment theory to the understanding of conduct problems during the preschool years, In. J. Belsky and T. Nezworski (eds.) *Clinical Implications of Attachment*, Hillsdale: Lawrence Erlbaum.

Guirdham, M. (1990) *Interprersonal Skills at Work*, Hemel Hempstead: Prentice Hall.

Hall, C., (1995) Parents may back bullying, *Independent on Sunday,* 2nd. April, 1995.

Harding, C. (1983) Acting with intention: A framework for examining the development of the intention to communicate, In. L. Feagans, C. Garvey and R. Golinkoff (eds.) *The Origins and Growth of Communication*, Norwood, N.J: Ablex.

Hargreaves, D.H. (1980) A sociological critique of individualism in education, *British Journal of Educational Studies*, 28, 187-198.

Herbert, M. (1985) *Caring For Your Children: A Practical Guide*, Oxford: Blackwell.

Herrenkohl, E.C., Herrenkohl, R.C. and Toedter, L.J. (1983) Perspectives on the inter-generational transmission of abuse, In. D. Finkelhor, R.J. Gelles, G.T. Hotaling and M.A. Straus (eds.) *The Dark Side of Families*, Beverley Hills: Sage.

Hoberman, H.M. (1990) Study group report on the impact of television violence on adolescence, *Journal of Adolescent Health Care*, 11, 45- 49.

Hofferman, M. L. (1977) Sex differences in empathy and related behaviours, *Psychological Bulletin*, 84, 712-722.

Hudson, B.C. and Macdonald, G.M. (1986) Behavioural Social Work: An Introduction, London: Macmillan.

Iscoe, I., Hill, F.E., Harman, M., and Coffmann, D. Telephone counselling via cassette tapes, *Journal of Counselling Psychology*, 26, 166-168.

Jennings, K, Stragg, V. and Palay, A. (1988) Assessing support networks: Stability and evidence for convergence on divergent validity, *American Journal of Community Psychology*, 16, 793-809.

Jesness, C.F. (1966) *The Jesness Inventory Manual*, Palo Alto, CA Consulting Psychologists' Press.

Josephson, W.L. (1987) Television violence and children's aggression: Testing the priming, social script and disinhibition restrictions, *Journal of Personality and Social Psychology*, 53, 882-890.

Jouriles, E.N., Murphy, C.M., Farris, A.M., Smith, D.A., Richters, J.E. and Waters, E. (1991) Marital adjustment, parental disagreements about child rearing and behaviour problems in boys: Increasing the specificity of the marital assessment, *Child Development*, 62, 1424-2433.

Kagan, J. (1974) Developmental and methodological considerations in the study of aggression. In. J. deWit and W.W. Hartup (eds.) *Determinants and Origins of Aggressive Behaviour*, The Hague: Mouton.

Katcher, M.L., (1987) Prevention of tap water scald burns: evaluation of a multi media injury control program, *American Journal of Public Health*, 3, 337-354.

Katz, I. and Bundy, A. (1994) A shepherd in search of a hook, *The Guardian*, 7th. April, p 2.

Kazdin, A.E. (1987) Treatment of antisocial behaviour in children: Current status and future direction, *Psychological Bulletin*, 102, 187-203.

Kelly, E. and Cohn, T. (1988). *Rasicm in Schools: New Research Evidence*. Stoke-on-Trent: Trentham.

Klinner, M., Campos, J.J., Sorce, J., Emde, R. and Svejda, M. (1983) Emotions as behaviour regulators: Social referencing in infancy. In. R. Plutchik and H. Kellerman (eds.) *Emotions in Early Development: Vol 2: The Emotions*, New York: Academic Press.

Kopp, C. (1982) The antecedents of self-regulation, *Developmental Psychology*, 18, 199-214.

Lamborn, S.D., Mounts, M.S., Steinberg, L. and Dornbusch, S.M. (1991) Patterns of competence and adjustment among adolescents from authoritative, authoritarian, indulgent and neglectful families, *Child Development*, 1049-1065.

Landy, S. and Peters, R.DeV. (1990) Identifying and treating hyperaggressive preschoolers, *Infants and Young Children*, 3, 24-28.

Landy, S. and Peters, R.DeV (1992) Aggressive conduct during the preschool years, In. R. DeV. Peters, R.L. McMahon. V.L. Quinsey (eds.) *Aggression and Violence Throughout the Life Span*, Newbury Park: Sage.

Lazar, B.A. (1994) Why social work should care: Television violence and children, *Child and Adolescent Social Work Journal*, 11, 3-19.

Lempers, J.D., Clark-Lempers, D. and Simons, R.L. (1989) Economic hardship, parenting and distress in adolescence, *Child Development*, 60, 25-39.

Levy, A.S. and Stokes, R.C. (1987) Effects of a healthpromotion advertising campaign on sales of ready-to-eat cereals, *Public Health Reports*, 102, 398-403.

Lipsitt, L. (1990) Fetal development in the drug age, *Child Behaviour and Development Letter,* 6, 1-3.

Lipsitt, P.D., Buka, S. and Lipsitt, L. (1990) Early intelligence scores and subsequent delinquency, *American Journal of Family Therapy*, 18, 197-208.

Loeber, R. (1991) Antisocial behaviour: More endurable than changeable? *Journal of the American Academy of Child and Adolescent Psychiatry*, 30, 393-397.

Luzio-Lockett, A. (1995) Enhancing relationships within organisations, *Employee Counselling Today*, 7, 12-22.

Lyman, D., Moffit, T.E. and Stouthamer-Loeber, M. (1993) Explaining the relation between IQ and delinquency: Class, race, test motivation, school failure or self-control? *Journal of Abnormal Psychology*, 102 (4) 552.

Lytton, J. (1990) Child and parent effects in boys' conduct disorder: A reinterpretation, *Developmental Psychology*, 26, 683-697.

MacDonald, K. and Parke, R.D. (1984) Bridging the gap: Parent-child play interaction and peer interactive competence, *Child Development*, 55, 1265-1277.

McIlwraith, R.D., (1987) Community Mental Health and the Mass Media in Canada, *Canada's Mental Health*, September.

McBrian, J. and Foxen, T. (1981) *Training Staff in Behavioural Methods: The EDY Programme*, Manchester: Manchester University Press.

McCord, J.B. and Packwood, W.T. (1973) Crisis centres and hotlines: A survey, *Personnel and Guidance Journal*, 51, 723-728.

McGulliciddy-deLisi, A.V. (1982) Parental beliefs about developmental processes, *Human Development*, 2, 5, 192-200.

McNiff, (1988) *Action Research, Principles and Practice*, London: Macmillan.

McGuire, W.J., (1984) Public communication, a strategy for inducing health promoting behaviour change. *Preventive Medicine*, 18, 299-319.

McQuire, J. and Richmond, N. (1986) The prevalence of behaviour problems in three types of pre-school groups, *Journal of Child Psychology and Psychiatry*, 27, 455-472.

Mahler, M., Pine, F. and Bergman, A. (1975) *The Psychological Birth of the Human Infant*, New York: Basic Books.

Main, M., Kaplan, M. and Cassidy, J. (1985) Security in infancy, childhood and adulthood: A more to the level of representation, In. I. Bretherton and E. Waters (eds.) Growing points of attachment theory and research, *Monographs of the Society for Research in Child Development*, 50 (1-2, Serial No. 209) 66-102.

Maines, B. and Robinson, G. (1992) *Michael's Story: The No Blame Approach*, Bristol: Lame Duck Publishing.

Manning, M., Heron, J. and Marshall, T. (1978) Styles of hostility and social interaction at the nursery, at school and at home, In. L.A. Hersov and M. Berger (eds.) *Aggression and Anti-social Behaviour in Childhood and Adolescence*, Oxford: Pergamon.

Marcus, R., Roke, E. and Bruner, C. (1985) Verbal and non-verbal empathy and prediction of social behaviour of young children, *Perceptual and Motor Skills*, 60, 299-309.

Maslow, A.H. (1954) *Motivation and Personality*, New York: Harper and Row.

Messner, S. (1986) Television violence and violent crime: An aggregate analysis, *Social Problems*, 33, 218-235.

Miller, P. and Sperry, L. (1987) The socialisation of anger and aggression. *Merrill Palmer Quarterly*, 33, 1-31.

Monroe, R.R. (1974) Maturational lag in central nervous system development a a partial explanation of episodic violent behaviour, In. J. deWit and W.W. Hartup (eds.) *Determinants and Origins of Aggressive Behaviour*, The Hague: Mouton.

Moran, S., Smith, P.K., Thompson, D.A. and Whitney, I. (1993) Ethnic differences in experiences of bullying: Asian and White children, *British Journal of Educational Psychology*, 63, 431-440.

Olweus, D. (1978) *Aggression in the schools: Bullies and whipping boys*, Washington DC: Hemisphere Press.

Olweus, D. (1978) Stability of aggressive reaction problems in males: A review, *Psychological Bulletin*, 86, 852-875.

Olweus, D. (1980) Familial and temperamental determinants of aggressive behaviour in adolescent boys: A causal analysis, *Developmental Psychology*, 16, 644-660.

Olweus, D. (1993) *Bullying at School: What We Know and What We Can Do*, Oxford, Blackwell.

Ovrebo, B., Ryan, M., Jackson, K. andHutchinson, K. (1994) The Homeless Parental Program: A model for empowering homeless pregnant women, *Health Education Quarterly*, 21, 187-198.

Paik, H. and Comsock, G. (1994) The effects of television violence on antisocial behaviour: A meta-analysis, *Communication Research*, 21, 516-546.

Parens, H. (1979) *The Development of Aggression in Early Childhood*, New York: Jason Aronson.

Parke, R.D. and Slaby, R.G. (1983) The development of aggression, In. P.H. Maissen, (ed.) *Handbook of Child Psychology* (4th ed.) Vol 4 547-642, New York: John Wiley.

Patterson, G.R. (1982) *Coercive Family Process*, Eugene, Oregon: Castilia.

Patterson, G.R. (1986) Maternal rejection: Determinant or product of deviant clutch behaviour, In. W. Hartup and Z. Rubin (eds.) *Relationships and development*, Hithdale, New York: McGraw Hill.

Perry, D.G., Kusal, S.J. and Perry, L.C. (1988) Victims of peer aggression, *Developmental Psychology*, 801-814.

Pikas, A. (1989) A pure concept of mobbing gives the best results for treatment, *School Psychology International,* 10, 95 -104.

Power, T. and Chapieski, M. (1986) Childrearing and impulse control in toddlers: A naturalistic investigation, *Developmental Psychology*, 22, 271-275.

Priestley, P., McGuire, J., Flegg, D., Helmsley, V. and Welham, D. (1978) *Social Skills and Personal Problem Solving: A Handbook of Methods*, London: Tavistock.

Pulkkinen, L. and Tremblay, R.E. (1992) Patterns of boys' social adjustment in two cultures and at different ages: A longitudinal perspective, *International Journal of Behavioural Development*, 15, 527-553.

Ramsey, P. (1987) Possession episodes in young children's social interactions,* Journal of Genetic Psychology*, 148, 315-324.

Randall, P.E. (1995) *Training Counsellors of the Victims of Harassment and Bullying*, Hull: The University of Hull.

Randall, P.E. (1991) *The Prevention of School-Based Bullying,* Hull: The University of Hull.

Randall, P.E. (1993) Tackling aggressive behaviour in the under-fives, *Professional Care of Mother and Child*, 3, 178-180.

Randall, P.E. (1995) Beyond the school gates, *Special Children.*

Randall, P.E. and Donohue, M. (1993) Tackling bullying as a community, *Child Education*, 70, 78-80.

Reid, J.B. (1986) Social intervention patterns in families of abused and non-abused children, In. C. Zahn-Waxler, E.M. Cummings, and R.Zanotti (eds.) *Altruism and Aggression, Biological and Social Origins*, Cambridge, Cambridge University Press.

Reid, W.J. and Epstein, L. (1972) *Task-Centered Practice*, New York: Columbia University Press.

Reid, W.J. and Schyne, A. (1968) *Brief and Extended Casework*, New York: Columbia University Press.

Richards, M. (1995) Family relations, *The Psychologist*, 8, 70-72.

Richman, N., Stevenson, J. and Tamplin, P. (1985) Prevalence of behaviour problems of three-year-old children: An epidemiological study in a London Borough, *Journal of Child Psychology and Child Psychiatry*, 16, 222-287.

Rigby, K. (1994) Psychosocial functioning in families of Australian adolescent school children involved in bully/victim problems, *Journal of Family Therapy*, 16, 173-187.

Rigby, K. and Slee, P.T. (1991) Bullying among Australian school children: Reported behaviour and attitudes towards victims, *Journal of Social Psychology*, 131, 615-627.

Roberto, K.A., Van-Amburg, S. and Orleans, M. (1994) The caregiver empowerment project: Developng programs within rural communities, *Activities, Adaptivity and Ageing*, 18, 1 -12.

Rodgers, A.V. (1993) The assessment of variables related to the parenting behaviour of mothers with young children, *Child and Youth Services Review*, 15(5) 385-402.

Roland, E. (1989) Bullying: The Scandinavian research tradition, In D.P. Tattum and D.A. Lane (eds.). *Bullying In Schools*. Stoke-on-Trent: Trentham.

Rubin, K.H. and Mills, S.L. (1992) Parent's thoughts about children's socially adaptive and maladaptive behaviours: Stability, change and individual differences, In. I. Sigel, J. Goodnow, and A.W. McGullicuddy-deLisi (eds.) *Parental Belief Systems*, Hillsdale: Lawrence Erlbaum.

Rubin, K.H., Mills, R.S.L. and Rose-Krasnor, L. (1989) Maternal beliefs and children's social competence, In. B. Schneider, G. Attili, J. Nadel and R. Weissberg (eds.) *Social Competence in Developmental Perspective*, Netherlands: Kluwer.

Sharp, S., Cowie, H. and Smith, P.K. (1994) Responding to bullying behaviour. In S. Sharp and P.K. Smith (eds) *Tackling Bullying in Your School: A Practical Handbook for Teachers*. London: Routledge.

Sharp, S. and Smith, P.K. (1994) *Tacking Bullying in Your School: A Practical Handbook for Teachers*. London: Routledge.

Sharp, S. and Thompson, D. (1992) Sources of stress: A contrast between pupil perspectives and teachers' perspectives, *School Psychology International*, 13, 229-242.

Smith, P.K. and Sharp, S. (1994) *School Bullying*, London: Routledge.

Sigel, I.E. (1982) The relationship between parental distancing strategies and the child's cognitive behaviour, In. L.M. Lavsa and I.E. Sigel (eds.) *Families as Learning Environments for their Children*, New York: Plenum.

Speltz, M. (1990) The treatment of preschool conduct problems, In. M. Greenberg, D. Cicchetti, and E.C. Cummings, (eds.) *Attachment in the Preschool Years*, Chicago, University of Chicago Press.

Sroufe, L.A. (1988) The role of infant-caregiver attachment in development, In. J. Belsky and T. Nezworski (eds.) *Clinical Implications of Attachment*, Hillsdale: Lawrence Erlbaum.

Stein, D.M. and Lambert, M.J. (1984) Telephone counselling and crisis intervention: A review, *American Journal of Community Psychology*, 12, 101-126.

Steinberg, L., Lamborn, S.D., Dornbusch, S.M. and Darling, N. (1992) Impact of parenting practices on adolescent achievement: Authoritative parenting, school involvement and encouragement to succeed, *Child Development*, 63, 1266-1281.

Stephenson, P. and Smith, D. (1987) Anatomy of a playground bully, *Education*, 18 September, 236-237.

Stern, D. (1985) *The Interpersonal World of the Infant*, New York: Basic Books.

Straus, M.A. (1983) Ordinary violence, child abuse and wife beating: What do they have in common? In. D. Finkelhor, R.J. Gelles, G.T. Hotaling and M.A. Straus (eds.) *The Dark Side of Families*, Beverley Hills: Sage.

Szegal, B. (1985) Stages in the development of aggressive behaviours in early childhood, *Aggressive Behaviour*, 11, 315-321.

Tizard, B., Blatchford, P., Burke,J., Farquhar, C. and Plewis, I. (1988) *Young Children at School in the Inner City*, Hillsdale: Lawrence Erlbaum.

Tronick, E.Z. (1989) Emotions and emotional communication in infants, *American Psychologist*, 44, 112-119.

Troyna, B. and Hatcher, R. (1992) *Racism in Children's Lives: A Study of Mainly White Primary Schools*. London: Routledge.

Turkel, S.B. and Eth, S. (1990) Psychopathological response to stress and post-traumatic stress disorder in children and adolescents, In L.E. Arnold (ed.) *Childhood Stress*, New York: Wiley.

Tyhurst (1951) Individual Reactions to Community Disaster. *American Journal of Psychiatry*, 1071, 764-769.

Van Reenan, L. (1992) Bullying in community and youth work, *Youth and Policy*, 38, 16-23.

Vaughn, B., Kopp. C. and Kurakow, J. (1984) The emergence and consolidation of self control from 18 to 30 months of age: Normative trends and individual differences, *Child Development*, 55, 990-1004.

Walker, K.B. and Morley, D.D., (1991) Attitudes and parental factors as intervening variables in the television violence-aggression relation, *Communication Research Reports*, 8, 41-47.

Weiss, B., Dodge, K.A. Bates, J.E. and Pettit, G.S. (1992) Some consequences of early harsh discipline: Child aggression and maladaptive information processing, *Child Development*, 63, 1321-1335.

White, J., Moffit, T., Earls, F., Robins, L., and Silva, P. (1990). Preschool predictors of conduct disorder, *Criminology*, 28, 507-533.

Windle, M. (1992) A longitudinal study of stress suffering for adolescent problem behaviours, *Developmental Psychology*, 28, 522-530.

Index

The words bullying, schools, teachers, parents, behaviour, community and project are *de facto* key words throughout this book. They are not indexed as they occur, explicitly or implicitly, on virtually every page.